# GATHERING RAGE

# GATHERING RAGE

## The Failure of
## Twentieth Century
## Revolutions to Develop a
## Feminist Agenda

## by Margaret Randall

**Monthly Review Press**

*Library of Congress Cataloging-in-Publication Data*

Randall, Margaret, 1936-
    Gathering rage : the failure of twentieth century revolutions
  to develop a feminist agenda / Margaret Randall.
        p.    cm.
    ISBN 0-85345-860-X : $28.00. — ISBN 0-85345-861-8 (pbk.) : $12.00
    1. Women's rights—Nicaragua—Case studies. 2. Women's rights—
Cuba—Case studies. 3. Women and socialism—Nicaragua—Case studies.
4. Women and socialism—Cuba—Case studies. 5. Feminism—
Nicaragua—Case studies. 6. Feminism—Cuba—Case studies.
    I. Title.
    HQ1236.5.N5R36    1992
    305.42'097285—dc20                                     92-29712
                                                              CIP

Monthly Review Foundation
122 West 27th Street
New York, NY 10001

10 9 8 7 6 5 4 3 2 1

# CONTENTS

*For all my feminist sisters and brothers*
*who share the dream of justice,*
*and for Ruth Hubbard: thank you.*

For women, the need and desire to nurture each other is not pathological but redemptive, and it is within that knowledge that our real power is rediscovered. It is this real connection which is so feared by a patriarchal world. For it is only under a patriarchal structure that maternity is the only social power open to women.

**—Audre Lorde**[1]


The obstacles are ideological rather than political. It is the expression of patriarchal thought that permeates everything, that makes for a one-sided vision of society . . . Not only is there tremendous ignorance of a feminist agenda, but when it is addressed it is addressed paternalistically, condescendingly, in welfare terms. We are lacking in profound and serious reflection on the subject.

**—Sofia Montenegro, Nicaragua**[2]

# TO SET A CONTEXT . . .

I began writing this essay at a terrible time. Those of us who engage in the ongoing struggle for justice began to experience our world disintegrating as we watched. Of course the balance of power, globally, has been against us as long as we can remember. But recent events define a qualitatively different period.

President Bush's new world order becomes more and more entrenched, daily reaping a misery that begins to defy even our ability to name it. Here at home, Reaganomics continue to whittle away at people's lives, with ever-increasing numbers of homeless and hopeless on our streets. And these are not numbers; they are human beings, each with a story to tell.

So many of the goals we fought for and won in the

last several decades—civil rights, affirmative action, welfare, day care, choice—are being decimated by the conservative political agenda, which now includes an overwhelmingly conservative Supreme Court. And the brutal racism, sexism, homophobia, everyday violence and abuse—product and purveyor of these ills—are a backdrop to each new day's events. They imbue our times with a mean spiritedness rarely seen before. Many of us have been personally victimized by these horrors. And although we have learned to talk about them more explicitly, and in some cases heal from them more effectively, we have not even begun to disarticulate the systems that fuel them.

Then, just as capitalism begins to reach an all time low, the socialist dream of justice starts to unravel as well, and fast. Life in the socialist countries wasn't perfect; we knew that. But it offered the most palpable ideal for placing human need before profit. Each generation of rebels has suffered its betrayals and disillusionments. For our parents it was the revelation of Stalin's crimes, in the documents of the Twentieth Congress. For me and many of my comrades, the terrible understanding of what was going on in Cambodia (or Kampuchea, as we preferred to name that country) was the first sign that lies could be told in the name of "socialism," lies monumental enough to force a questioning of every formula.

Still, there continues to be a reality and a purpose to our struggle. We experience some degree of collective depression or rage, but not defeat. We understand the interests being served through the type of reporting engaged in by most of the Western media, and that although there is a painful story to tell, we are hardly receiving the real one. Some of us have known socialism first hand. We believe, I continue to believe, that a type of egalitarian society is the only remedy to the increasing injustice, misery, and degradation suffered by the vast majority of peoples.

This is the memory I hold onto. I've been privileged to live and participate in several societies where equality was the goal. I was in Cuba from 1969 through 1980, visited the Socialist Republic of North Vietnam in the fall of 1974, and then there was Nicaragua: not a socialist country, but certainly one where for ten years a people in government attempted to make life better for the majority. I worked in Nicaragua for part of 1979 and it was my home from the end of 1980 to the beginning of 1984. In each of these places I experienced alternatives to an abusive exercise of power. People living and working in touch with their needs, people mandated to fulfill those needs, is exciting beyond description. Perhaps it must be lived to be fully understood.

So, as news of the "death of socialism" bombarded our senses, I felt it as an agony but not a death knell. I was aware of the revolutionary errors, of the danger of corruption as well as of the well-intentioned mistakes. And I also knew, because it had affected my life and the lives of those I love, what the weight of constant hostile pressure from a world power determined to destroy such experiments could mean. These revolutions continue to be a part of our collective memory, I thought; their lessons will have an important place in the years to come.

Then too, I am a woman and a feminist. The feminist wave of the late 1960s and early 1970s swept me up, permanently empowering me to see myself—and the world—with new eyes. As a woman, as a feminist, the current contradictions began calling up a very particular rage. Increasingly, I have come to believe that a fundamental error of twentieth century revolutions has been their inability—or unwillingness—to develop a feminist agenda. And this is what I will explore in the pages that follow.

Back in the 1970s I said socialism and feminism need one another. I still believe that. But history has pushed me considerably in my understanding of how complex, and essential, such a coming together must be. Power is a feminist issue, perhaps the central feminist issue. As I began to work on this essay, as I gave it to friends to read and engaged people in a discussion of these ideas, I quickly realized how separate, how *separatist*, most of us still are.

The majority of white and/or privileged women in the United States and Europe who call ourselves feminists know and care little about the revolutionary experiments, assuming they have nothing to do with us. Many feminists of color within the oppressor nations—African Americans, Chicanas, Latinas, Native Americans, Asian Americans, and others—are too preoccupied with the dire problems of their communities to worry about socialism somewhere in the world. Or, fearing an ideology they have been told divides them from their brothers in arms, they may refuse to identify themselves as feminists.

As a group, the same can be said for the men and women who call ourselves revolutionaries. Traditionally, we have understood feminism, when we have understood it at all, as *one component* in the struggle for a more just society. A component to be incorporated into the struggle itself, or one to which we may be able to turn our attention (many secretly hoping that that won't be necessary, at least during their lifetimes!) only after the decisive battles have been won. A component, not an integral part of the vision. You will see, as you read this essay, that I believe this understanding to be profoundly skewed.

Consequently, several of those who read successive drafts suggested I write two separate pieces: one aimed at explaining to feminists the socialism I have experienced; the other speaking to socialists and those who call themselves revolutionaries about the importance of a feminist point of view. That might have been an easier way of doing it, but I don't think it would have served my purpose. If, as I believe, we must develop a new language with which to name new concepts, then here, too, I want to claim my voice—not only by calling forth the old forms but by helping to invent the new.

We must also be willing to ask more aggressive questions. Is socialism, as we have conceived it, the answer to society's ills? Can a socialist model take into account and fully incorporate the ways in which we so clearly must readdress *gender,* race, and ethnicity in our own vision of social change?

During the course of this writing, something happened (as it always does) that greatly helped me to understand what is at stake. Here is the story. My son, now in his early thirties, unexpectedly retrieved a ragged notebook, a diary he wrote during his thirteenth year. He had forgotten its existence; I hadn't been aware of it at all. Gregory lived with us in Cuba at that time, attending a boarding school reserved for the brightest and most enthusiastic students. His diary entries speak of his relationships with friends and family, falling in love, intellectual and manual work, local and international politics.

Let me tell you a little about what Gregory was like back then. He was intellectual and imaginative. His readings that year included Brazilian novelist Jorge Amado's *Captains of the Sand,* Anatoli Marchenko's *Pedagogical Poem*, *With Uncle Ho* (about Ho Chi Minh), and *Stalin on Lenin*. He played a lot of chess, although several years earlier—fearing he wasn't athletic enough—he had enrolled himself in one of Cuba's national sports schools, where he remained until he became a better than average swimmer. During the time covered by this diary, Gregory also experienced what he then described as his "sexual coming of age," that is, his first ejaculation (duly noted in an almost illegible hand). He had crushes on a number of female classmates. And he wrote a lot of poetry.

As we read the diary and remembered (from our differing points of view) the people, places, and events, both of us were powerfully struck by a central contradiction. On the one hand, there is an openness, a devotion, and a confidence in the possibility of a better world, and in a young person's ability to take an active part in its construction. Everything was couched in revolutionary terms. Particularly at the beginning of that year, the terms and their implementation were accepted without question.

As was true of all Cuban students from middle-level education on up, Gregory was engaged in production work as well as with his studies. The school had its own factories and agricultural areas. He was a student guide, which meant that he frequently led foreign dignitaries through the buildings and grounds; his diary records the visits of Mitterand, Brezhnev, and Boumedienne. Working with those in his group who ignored or spurned him as well as with friends, he tried to achieve collective goals, mediate problems, and speak out about issues and events in a deeply political way.

Gregory wrote of his struggle to help one classmate, in particular, out of semi-delinquency. He approached the problem by explaining to the boy that his conduct was "not revolutionary." It wasn't an easy task he'd set for himself. "This is a long pedagogical poem," he wrote of his effort, referring to Anatoli Marchenko's book by the same name.

There are dozens of Gregory's own poems in the diary. Most were written to revolutionary heroes or heroines, or to the events that gave them glory. The poems sing their praises in highly rhetorical terms—life, death, love, commitment, fear—all are rendered listless by virtue of the clichéd or barren voice. And this is the contradiction that jars the reader: the abundance of slogans and the flatness of language used to describe people and events so deeply felt. When problems are repressed and only the positive is worthy of mention, then the exciting becomes sterile on the page.

As a result this diary lacks even a glimmer of unique expression. My son and his friends were protagonists in an extraordinary human experience. They were capable, as young people are, of intense feeling, complex analysis, acute self-observation. Yet they were utterly unable to give true voice to that experience.

Not that his writing is devoid of process or progression. At one point about halfway through the notebook, Gregory writes: "I know I am not telling you [the diary] what I feel. I wish I could find the words to tell you what I feel." Toward the end, a slightly more critical stance becomes apparent. A language of greater substance begins to evolve. At the same time, some innocence is lost. But the distance between the life experience of an obviously sensitive young man and the language with which he is able to speak that experience is still striking.

It seems to me that it is precisely this distance that signals a problem central to the larger picture. Language itself (by which I mean a feeling/thinking language— original, creative, critical, poetic) emanating from the body as well as the mind, constitutes a way of seeing and understanding the world. If we are unable to develop language fully, we will never see and know what is possible. And any curtailment of this process acts as a brake upon the natural development of perceptivity, discernment, creativity, confidence in one's energies and strengths, and the capacity for critical thinking.

So how do we achieve a balance? The very simplicity of life, the interconnectedness of life and work so evident in the early years of the Cuban revolution, as well as a very real fear that the achievements would be attacked and destroyed, limited popular discourse. Yet as the revolution grew stronger and the possibility for a more complex discourse developed, much of what we know as revolution was swallowed up or lost. How to ·encourage the complexity while retaining the wonder?

Some form of socialist economics is necessary to the building of a society in which everyone contributes and everyone is cared for. Sacrifice, often tremendous sacrifice, is a part of it all. A feminist vision is essential to develop the creative energy needed to take on that sacrifice. Feminism is all about creative change. It might well provide the balance and the bridge capable of advancing changes that will last. I say this because feminism puts us in touch with ourselves, with our bodies as well as with our minds; a feminist vision honors feeling and thought *and the way the two connect.*

For this reason I do not say: social revolution needs feminism as simply one more component, something to be added on or factored in. No. *If revolution incorporates feminism it will transform itself.* I believe that only through such a transformation will revolutionary change be capable of meeting the broadest range of people's needs. And I believe it is only through such a transformation that those affected will truly defend the revolution.

This is very much what I want to explore in these pages. If there is repetition, if the discourse seems spiral or even circular at times, if you think two differently directed essays would have been more satisfying than one, please understand that weaving a single fabric is what this is about. If those of you who identify more as feminists find the details of revolution weighty or boring, be patient. What has made people's lives better is worth reading about. And if those of you who identify more as socialists find yourself muttering *but we know this*, reconsider: what has happened in the proclamations, and even in the law, has not always been true in practice. In writing this essay, I am grateful to a number of friends and colleagues for their response to my ideas, for their own ideas, and for a great deal of rich discussion. Connie Adler, Karin Aguilar-San Juan, Miranda Bergman, Kathy Boudin, Blanche Cook, Clare Coss, Michele Costa, John Crawford, Kipp Dawson, Janice Gould, Minrose Gwin, Ruth Hubbard, Elizabeth Kennedy, Paul Lauter, Jack Levine, Jules Lobel, Janet Melvin, Gregory Randall, John Randall, Adrienne Rich, Ruth Salvaggio, Susan Sherman, and Patricia Clark Smith have given me valuable feedback. Thank you, all.

My women's writing group in Albuquerque, New Mexico, is always a source of strength. Audiences at the Gay Women's Alternative in New York City and Trinity College in Hartford, Connecticut, where I read from earlier drafts, were helpful in raising additional questions and challenging some of my assumptions. My life partner, Barbara Byers, is my strongest critic and most consistent supporter; our respect for one another's work and the life we share make everything possible.

# 1
# WHERE IT SUDDENLY
# CAME CLEAR . . .

Today's school children, and yesterday's as well, learn a mutilated history because women are not included, but also because there's no analysis of the effect of how our culture has been damaged. Our history books don't tell us how our ancestors' customs were destroyed, how each set of colonizers punished the "heretics" because they saw the devil in every social, familial, or sexual practice that didn't fit their rigid puritanical values. . . . The silence about our past obliges us to write our own history, and we must remember: the present is tomorrow's past. We must not allow a sexist vision of history to deny our lives to our great granddaughters . . .

**—an editorial in *La boletina*, Managua**[1]

The scene is a solidarity conference in Managua, October 1991. A year and a half after its electoral defeat, the Sandinista National Liberation Front (FSLN) has invited supporters of Nicaragua's revolution to meet and analyze its current situation, and to talk about future strategies.[2] We have come from Latin America, the United States and Canada, Europe, even Asia and Australia. I see no one from Africa. Women and men seem equally represented.

This is my first trip back to Nicaragua since I left in 1984. Recognition and anguish wash over me in alternating waves of feeling. Memory plays strange tricks. The wet heat is familiar, comforting. Squeezing a bit of lime onto a steak that I know represents sacrifice in this country today reminds me of the stores filled with produce so few can buy. An immense figure of Sandino takes me by surprise.[3] The terrible sense of loss seems most immediately evident to me in the dozens of murals—painted by artists from all over the world—that have been erased as if their beauty never existed here.

The solidarity conference was a different experience for each of us, depending perhaps most of all on our age and the length of time we had been involved with the Nicaraguan revolutionary movement. Filling out my registration form and coming to the question, "In what year did you begin your support work for the FSLN?" I realized as I wrote "1971" that it's been twenty years.

Twenty years, first of mundane work, a sort of tenacious patience, then of an involvement that it used to surprise me was shared by so few, the grandiose feats of a David confronting Goliath, the terrible deaths of comrades, and finally victory in 1979: so sudden as to seem almost unreal. And then there was no stopping, even to rest. Many revolutionaries have spoken or written that the task of remaking society is infinitely more difficult than winning a war of liberation.

At this conference a cheerful young woman held my attention. Wearing a red and black neckerchief, she looked in her early twenties. Michele Costa, of the Nicaraguan Network, told me that she is from Idaho, a farm worker whose parents are Republicans and who calls the Network at least once or twice a week to offer help with one task or another. When Sandinista dignitaries come to the United States on speaking tours, this young woman sends them little gifts, handmade by her and her friends in the country's heartland. I felt a mixture of gratitude and anxiety for this woman's eagerness and trust. Despite a few obvious differences, she might have been me two decades before. At the conference this young woman sat rapt, intent on every word.

Some of us, although attentive and deeply moved, were not so rapt. We had more questions than answers. We expected at least some of the answers to come from the members of the FSLN's national directorate, lined up facing us at the first plenary session and at most of those that followed. Tomás Borge was there, *old man* of the Sandinista experience, lone survivor among the visionaries who founded the FSLN in 1960; Bayardo Arce, with his brilliant discourse, alcoholic gaze, and macho ways; Henry Ruíz, a serious statesman who now handles solidarity, led most of the conference discussions; Luís Carrión, whom I have long considered one of the FSLN's finest leaders; Sergio Ramírez, once vice president, new to the directorate, complex and profound in his analysis. No women.

Ex-President Daniel Ortega appeared at the closing plenary and delivered a speech that was little more than a string of slogans. He sounded as if he might still be running for office. I left the room halfway through his speech, hurt and angry. Daniel's face seemed set in a kind of death mask, perhaps a year and a half old. I reminded myself that many of the revolutionaries who have given lifetimes of energy to this struggle, and who have seen ten years of superhuman effort disintegrate at the polls, must still be suffering the shock of loss and disbelief. There was the terrible absence of Carlos Núñez, perhaps the purest and most thoughtful of the directorate members, who died less than a year ago at the age of forty. And still, there were no women.

Suddenly, these were all just men. Men without the inspiring uniforms of their still extraordinary campaign. Political leaders who had waged a guerrilla war with cunning and courage, often with innovative and exceptional skill, and who went on to tackle the running of their country with varying degrees of competency. Most are authoritarian in manner; several are womanizers, in the crudest sense of that term. Only one, perhaps two, have the slightest interest in or respect for a feminist agenda. I do not know if any of them understands a feminist agenda as something beyond the proverbial "equal rights for women."

The second morning, during a session programmed for the discussion of a variety of issues, Michele Costa and I decided to accept the conference invitation for people to come to the mike with questions. Our long working relationships with the FSLN, and with Nicaraguan women, had made us attentive to concerns for both. Together we walked to the front of the assembly. Michele spoke first, addressing women's role in the FSLN and asking what plans the party has for implementing the impressive feminist project that was outlined (in very general terms) in the final document of its recent congress.[4]

Michele did not publicly question the congress's

failure to elect Commander Dora María Téllez to its national directorate.[5] We had talked beforehand and decided that airing the question in this forum might have been disrespectful of the party's internal decision-making process. But she noted that much of the solidarity constituency in the United States is female, that much of it is feminist in outlook, and that there is concern about deepening the process of incorporating women into positions of political power which the Sandinista revolution so clearly initiated throughout the 1970s and early 1980s. And she had a concrete proposal, reflecting a joint collaboration with women in the FSLN.[6]

I followed Michele's words with a few of my own about what we mean when we speak of a feminist agenda. I wanted to make it clear that we weren't talking about some limited and misleading something called the "woman problem." We are talking about a way of looking at the world, with half the population resituated in our rightful cultural and political space, a humanization of power and power relations, full participation, true revolutionary democracy.

As I finished I could feel a shudder of discomfort running along that row of men who looked down on the assembly, and perhaps some discomfort among the conferees as well. Luís Carrión took the mike to respond to Michele's and my questions. And surprisingly, because I know Carrión as an intelligent and responsive person, his answer was not what we'd hoped for.

What he said was that work with women will continue. And that if we wanted to be involved with that work, all we had to do was contact the various women's organizations: AMNLAE, the women's commissions of the peasant and union movements, among others.[7] I fought to dispel a "women's auxiliary" image from my mind. The old "we" and "they" seemed very much alive. We interpreted this response as a polite way of saying that the FSLN's national leadership really isn't all that concerned about a feminist agenda.

We were outraged, saddened. Michele returned to the mike and said that if this was the answer the FSLN's national directorate had for women in the U.S. solidarity movement, then she would certainly transmit it to her constituency back home. "But," she added, "it's not going to be an answer we find satisfactory." A brief exchange followed in which Carrión said that he "hadn't meant . . . that of course . . . " And we all moved on to other issues.

Among revolutionary organizations internationally, the Sandinista National Liberation Front *is* a political party concerned with women's participation. What about the struggles of the late 1960s and 1970s, when Nicaraguan women inside the organization battled with their men over a gendered division of labor in political and military roles, equal rights not *after* but *during* the war? What about the women—dozens, even hundreds of them—who became military officers and then political leaders in the new revolutionary government? What about the public debates on feminist issues? I had witnessed them, participated in them, when I lived in Managua throughout the early 1980s.

The fact that there is no widespread understanding of a feminist agenda, we reminded ourselves, doesn't preclude an attempt to grapple with the issue. After the session at which we challenged the directorate, Michele and I were given the opportunity to discuss our concerns with Henry Ruíz.[8] After I left, Michele then met with Luís Carrión. We agreed to make some study materials available to the FSLN leadership in Managua and to maintain periodic contact for follow-up. More importantly, the FSLN recognized the importance of reassessing a woman's position in the Nicaraguan political process, and took the first steps toward organizing a resource group of Sandinista women who are feminists. It will be interesting to see how these efforts develop. This is more than we expected, and perhaps more than most movements have been willing to commit themselves to, when it comes to a feminist vision.

I continue to be engaged, involved, and watchful but I am also angry and committed to the unending struggle to move women everywhere back into the center of our lives and history. Long before my return to Managua in 1991, I was so engaged and I imagine I will be so as long as I breathe and do battle for our lives. But much more to the point is the commitment of our Nicaraguan sisters. In today's Managua I found an explosion of feminist power.

In this book I want to explore the relationship between a feminist agenda and socialist revolution as we have known it. I want to understand why socialism—the only political system in my lifetime that has been committed to equality and justice—has failed so miserably. One reason may be traced to capitalism's long-term and successful efforts at destabilization. But I believe there are also important lessons to be learned about inadequacies within the socialist experiments themselves.

As a socialist, I want to look critically at those inadequacies. I will make some general observations while focussing on the experiences of Nicaragua and Cuba, which I know from having lived in those countries, having participated in their revolutionary processes, and having written extensively about their women's lives. As a feminist, I want to look at socialism from a holistic and woman-centered perspective. This will not be a linear journey. Many of my questions as yet have no answers. I invite you to trust your memory and instinct, to put aside preconceived notions spawned in a world of disinformation, and to engage in a discussion that honors passion as well as reason.

Before going any further, I want to define feminism as I understand it. bell hooks offers a useful point of departure when she says: "Feminism is not simply a struggle to end male chauvinism or a movement to ensure that women will have equal rights with men; it is a commitment to eradicating the ideology of domination that permeates Western culture on various levels— sex, race, and class, to name a few—and a commitment to reorganizing...society so that the self-development of people can take precedence over imperialism, economic expansion, and material desires."[9] I would add:

feminism is about memory, about re-inserting memory into history; about not repressing but confronting and making useful the painful memories that surface in our lives. It is about the conception and uses of power, about relationships in the human, animal, and natural worlds— who holds power and over whom. It requires rethinking and reorganizing both our notions of society and society itself, so that we all may make our unique contributions and participate to our fullest potential.

Feminism is a world view that also embraces ecological concerns, support for the life process in all its forms, and peace. Feminism is—joyously, sensually, painfully, courageously, creatively—about process as well as product. I mean that women are not afraid of pain; we have the courage to look at it and use it constructively. The feminism I'm talking about is an ongoing analysis rooted in experience, made by women out of and for our lives.

In this inquiry, I am really talking about two aspects of feminist concern. One is the obvious need for a broader and more deeply rooted inclusion of women in positions of political power. The other is what we might call the feminization of power itself. It is, in fact, a new and different notion of power than that which has limited and misdirected us to this point. These two aspects are dialectically intertwined. Feminism challenges absolutely everything about society—and about nature—that we have up to this point assumed as givens.

In an insightful statement about identity politics, June Jordan links sexuality, gender, and power in a way

I believe particularly useful to this discussion.[10] She points out that ". . . the Politics of Sexuality is the most ancient and probably the most profound arena for human conflict . . . deeper and more pervasive than any other oppression, than any other bitterly contested human domain . . . " Therefore, she reasons,

> [it] subsumes all of the different ways in which some of us seek to dictate to others of us what we should do, what we should desire, what we should dream about, and how we should behave ourselves, generally, on the planet. From China to Iran, from Nigeria to Czechoslovakia, from Chile to California, the politics of sexuality—enforced by traditions of state-sanctioned violence plus religion and the law—reduces to male domination of women, heterosexist tyranny, and among those of us who are in any case deemed despicable or deviant by the powerful, we find intolerance for those who choose a different, a more complicated—for example, an interracial or bisexual—mode of rebellion and freedom.

In this passage Jordan refuses to be limited by the right *or* left. Not just dark-skinned people, but people of mixed heritage and culture; not only those of us who are safely heterosexual or (unsafely) homosexual, but those who claim more than a single category of sexual affiliation: The Jew who loves herself and also loves the Palestinian people, the white revolutionary in South Africa, the mixed blood. For who among us identifies with the flatness of a single dimension?

Jordan moves past the ways in which patriarchy has organized the inequality of women to consider other unequal relations of power. Her observations are keenly applicable to the issues I wish to explore. When she concludes that "freedom is indivisible or it is nothing at all besides sloganeering and temporary, short-sighted, and short-lived advancement for a few," she pinpoints a *deviancy of the state* that, tragically, has plagued every one of the socialist experiments (as well, of course, as being one of the twisted underpinnings of capitalism).

Neither the capitalist societies that so falsely promise equality nor the socialist societies that promised equality and more have really taken on the challenge of feminism. We know how capitalism coopts every liberating concept, turning it into a slogan used to sell us what we do not need, where illusions of freedom replace the real thing. I now wonder if socialism's failure to make room for a feminist agenda—indeed, to embrace that agenda as it indigenously surfaces in each history and culture—is one of the reasons why socialism as a system could not survive.

I remain convinced that only some form of socialism will be capable of creating a society with justice, but not, however, until it is truly committed to the liberation of *all* peoples. What kind of socialism do I mean? No, not a utopian variety (which is what one is invariably accused of coddling when one strays from the classic concepts). Let me say for the record that I am talking about a system in which the means of production are controlled by the people who work to provide for everyone's needs, not for the boss's profit. From each according to their ability, to each according to their need—meaning not just shelter, food, health, education, but also the need for creativity, spontaneity, and joy. And meaning not only men, but women; not only a reorganization of production, but also of reproduction. Neither does my vision of socialism marginalize the children, the dark skinned, those who are differently abled, homosexuals, poets, seers, or crones. On the contrary, it must bring us all into the center—of society and of our lives.

Some see class alone as key to understanding relations of power. Some blame Lenin, in his theory of the party and concept of democratic centralism, for creating too vertical and elitist a structure. Some still speak of a revolution in permanence, and point to the kind of state capitalism that evolved in the Soviet Union as an example of how extreme centralism and bureaucracy can destroy the dream of equality. Some, myself among them, have been drawn back along the dual routes of what Raya Dunayevskaya called Marxist-Humanism and the Reichian method of breaking down the body's armor—in our search to insert more contemporary ideas of gender and race into a practical reexperiencing of knowledge and memory, thought and feeling, theory and action.[11]

Under capitalism, feminism has been an oppositional movement and thus outside the power structure; this has given it more room in which to struggle. And it has made important advances. Feminists in the United States, Canada, and some of the western European countries have developed theories of gender that today inform a range of multidisciplinary thinking. The United

States is also an exciting center for the development of feminist therapy, where a reassessment of incest and other sexual abuse issues has led to an attempt to heal the split between mind and body.

In the United States and Europe, African American and other feminists of color and lesbian-feminists have done important work in linking the strands of experience and thought from "third" to "first" world and back again.[12] Because of its oppositional nature in the capitalist context, however, feminism has also been less integral to the system, affecting far fewer women.

Under socialism, the stage should have been well set for feminist explorations. But something stood in the way. Why have these aspects of the theory and practice of liberation been stifled within the socialist experiments? In this book I have two concerns: the need for an autonomous feminist agenda, without which I am now convinced there can be no radical social change; and the centrality of a truly critical (pro-creative) process.

But first I would like to examine the participation of Nicaraguan women in the revolutionary conquest of political power, the changing relationship between their organizing efforts as women and the overall (mixed) movement, and how the Sandinista electoral defeat has shifted some of the emphasis and delineated more clearly the need for a feminist position.

# 2

# NICARAGUA:

# A RECENT CASE IN POINT . . .

During a revolutionary process ideas change. Women participated in our revolution, not in the kitchens but as fighters. As political leaders. This gives us a very different experience . . . A man would be hard put to lift a hand to hit or mistreat a woman combatant . . .

**—Dora María Téllez**[1]

In the early 1980s, I interviewed many women in Nicaragua who had participated in the war and then were actively engaged in the struggle of their revolution's first few years. We shared experiences, argued, raised our children together, worked alongside one another. I wrote extensively about these women's lives and their participation.[2] Now, returning to their country ten years later, I wanted to understand what they were thinking and feeling.

I wanted to know why so many women had voted against the Sandinistas. Was it because of the special anguish they suffered when a strangled economy couldn't put enough food on their tables and their sons and daughters continued to die in a war that seemed to have no end? Women always bear the most immediate burden when it comes to feeding their families. And analysts have been quick to point out that women, particularly, were exhausted by a war that had taken so many lives.

The FSLN was urged more than once to eliminate the draft, and shortly before the elections many hoped Daniel Ortega would announce that such was the case. He couldn't, or didn't. UNO's U.S.-designed and funded campaign promised that the election of a coalition backed by the United States would mean an end to the war, as well as provide millions of dollars to alleviate the economic crisis.[3] Clearly many women believed the promises.

I wanted to hear how these same women remembered feeling back in 1983 when the contra war took a turn for the worse and defense necessarily became the number one priority— for AMNLAE as well as for other mass organizations. At what point had despair or lethargy begun to alter conviction when feminist issues were discussed within the overall context of making revolution?

The origins of AMNLAE go back long before the Sandinista victory of 1979. The FSLN was founded in 1961, and nine years later, in the village of Juigalpa, Chontales, it made its first concerted effort to create a particular space for women. Gladys Báez, the first woman member of the rural guerrillas, called that 1969 meeting and ended up making a little speech to the other two women who showed up. Báez refers to that meeting as historic, when women came together for the first time to discuss their roles in the context of the country's political struggle. A decade later they and their brothers would win a war of liberation. By then the women's organization had gone through some evolution. Interestingly, in a move that would seem to bring things full circle, it is Gladys Báez who heads AMNLAE today.

After that first meeting and a number of other unsuccessful attempts, in the early 1970s the FSLN was finally able to organize women across class lines, in defense of political prisoners and related issues. That group, AMPRONAC (Association of Women Confronting the Problems of the Nation) would become the forerunner of AMNLAE.[4] Women from the cities, mostly professionals from the petty bourgeoisie, were its earliest members. Many were mothers of combatants who had been killed or were serving time in Somoza's jails. Gradually they reached out to peasant and working-class women who found it easier to come together as women than as workers or political cadre. That's when the organization became involved in strikes against price hikes and tax increases. When the war ended, AMPRONAC changed its name. In honor of a reticent young woman believed to have been the first female member of the FSLN to die in combat, it became the Luisa Amanda Espinosa Nicaraguan Women's Association, or AMNLAE.[5]

Like other popular sectors during the first years of revolutionary government, women experimented with

different organizational strategies. For a while they followed the Cuban model, a mass women's organization,
then discarded it in favor of a more mobile movement.
By 1983, in response to a directive handed down by the
FSLN, AMNLAE began putting most of its energy into
raising moral and material support for the mothers of
combatants.[6] The association urged mothers who were
reluctant to accept their sons' and daughters' recruit-
ment into the military, to understand that a broad-based
army was necessary for the defense of the nation.
Women were also encouraged to move into jobs left
vacant by husbands and brothers needed at the front.

I was still living in the country when the Sandinistas
instituted a compulsory draft in response to the build-up
of the war. I think back to the day when the AMNLAE
representative to the Council of State argued passionately that women be included in the draft. The FSLN opposed AMNLAE on this, arguing that social services
were still grossly insufficient and that women were
needed to care for their children at home. The party
believed that drafting women under such circumstances
would not have a liberating effect on their lives but
would increase their burden. The feminist position, on
the other hand, argued that as long as protective legislation was in effect, women would be discriminated
against. This was one of the few instances in which the
FSLN and AMNLAE opposed one another. The FSLN
won. But not very many years later even male conscrip-
tion became a point of contention, distancing women
from the revolution.

In those early years, public health statistics began showing illegal abortions to be a leading cause of death for women of child-bearing age. Many (including the Minister of Public Health and other officials) felt that AMNLAE should be fighting to legalize abortion. But in this war crisis situation, and faced with the opposition of the Catholic hierarchy, the group remained timid on the issue. Today members of AMNLAE admit that it was a mistake not to have confronted the church. A year and a half into this period of conservative government, the organization's campaign to legalize abortion is now underway.

But I'm getting ahead of my story. In April 1985, following a self-critical evaluation of its work, AMNLAE held a national assembly. Women from all over the country gathered in Managua to talk about their needs and projects. There was a general consensus that along with war work, more emphasis had to be placed on specifically feminist concerns. Sexuality, discrimination in the workplace, and abuse in the home were some of the issues that begged to be addressed. This was the high point in the Sandinistas' ability to link a feminist agenda to the broader social and political struggle. From that April assembly to a second in September of the same year, 40,000 women who had organized into 600 grassroots meetings were involved in a broad-based and democratic discussion of their problems.

The September assembly marked AMNLAE's real coming of age as an organization that had to be taken seriously by the party's mostly male leaders. In mass, women identified with the questions they were asking, the answers they arrived at, and the actions that resulted from such intense and largely nontraditional inquiry. They learned that the Nicaraguan labor force had become increasingly feminized in recent years, but that women's needs were being ignored where they worked. They found that 62 percent of the electorate was female, but that women's issues were not seen as a priority. Women played an extremely active part in writing the new constitution, which was eventually approved by the Council of State in 1987, and many of their demands were reflected in its text.

Of course war was still tearing the nation apart, and an intensification of the conflict left its indelible mark on everything that was attempted during those years. At times, the revolution's very survival seemed a miracle. Within the FSLN there were different opinions with regard to a feminist agenda. I think it is safe to say that a very small minority of the men who controlled the party really understood feminism. And accusations that feminist issues only serve to weaken unity, dividing people in times of crisis, produced a sense of guilt in many of the AMNLAE leaders themselves.

Nevertheless, there were always a few male leaders who continued to struggle from a feminist perspective. In September of 1986, for the first time since the revolution had taken power, woman's changing role was the subject of intense discussion within the predominantly male Sandinista Assembly. This was quickly reflected, at least in the rhetoric. Two months later, on November

8, in a public act commemorating the party's twenty-fifth anniversary, President Daniel Ortega addressed tens of thousands gathered to hear him at July Nineteenth Plaza. The audience grew silent when he read point number nine of the proclamation produced by the Assembly: "The FSLN commits itself to guaranteeing women's rights and to struggle energetically against the residual sexism inherited from our past." It was the first time sexism had been mentioned explicitly in such a speech.

On March 8, 1987, AMNLAE held its third national assembly, where three thousand delegates attended. There Bayardo Arce agreed that "Nicaraguan women have historically suffered a social discrimination that has placed them in a subordinate role." He, too, denounced "sexism, paternal irresponsibility, and those unfair laws and policies which, in the family as well as in the larger social sphere, are obstacles to women giving their full energies to the construction of a new way of life." Emphasis, of course, was still rather heavily placed on women helping to build the new society, not on the kind of new society needed for women's lives to be different.

In such a climate, other organizations under the auspices of the FSLN also began paying more attention to women's issues. The National Union of Farmers and Cattle Breeders (UNAG), the National Conference of Professionals (CONAPRO), the Field Workers Association (ATC), and other groups all established or strengthened existing women's commissions. Some progress was being made.

But this was all about our first aspect of feminist concern: the need to include more women in the country's political life. The issue of a feminization of power was not being addressed, or even articulated. And where their private lives were concerned, many of the male leaders, who so loudly proclaimed the need for women's equality, quite obviously lived by different standards. As they were prominent figures, and Managua is a very small city, their private lives inevitably became public. Indeed, Nicaragua is a small country, where a few large families include numerous members and people easily know one another—a phenomenon that has worked both for and against change. If the men who *talked* such a good line continued to live their male privilege to the hilt, what about the ordinary doctor or ditch digger who was unacquainted with such concepts? A very obvious double standard continued to exist when it came to female and male socialization and the acceptable roles for women and men. This double standard, which has been so obvious in terms of gender, has more recently given rise to accusations of a lack of moral integrity on the part of certain FSLN leaders in other areas as well.[7] Cracks in the ethical conduct of a party or movement may frequently be seen in terms of how that party or movement deals with women in society.

By June 1988, when AMNLAE called its leadership assembly, it was clear that the organization had lost a good deal of its popular appeal. Putting feminist issues on the political agenda *without explaining what these is-*

*sues have to do with changing society as a whole,* created a number of contradictory interpretations of the FSLN's proclamation among some female leaders as well as among the men.

Missing was a solid feminist analysis—and the official support for that analysis—that might have made the difference. From one popular or professional organization to another, from one region of the country to another, even within the various government ministries, there was more indecision and even backlash than there was encouragement for female autonomy. In September 1988, during its eleventh anniversary celebration, AMNLAE announced a plan of struggle and a political process among its members designed to democratically elect a new national executive. At stake was who would run the organization, and consequently which perspective would be emphasized. Once again women in the different sectors joined in heated discussions about their needs: workers, peasants, housewives, intellectuals, artists, women in the armed forces, and women on the mostly Miskito and Creole Atlantic coast. It's important to emphasize the genuine process of decentralization that was taking place within AMNLAE at the time. Electing its own executive would have been in sharp contrast with a history of the FSLN always choosing the women who would lead the organization at the national level.

But quite suddenly "the Sandinista National Liberation Front interrupted this democratic process [which] was left unfinished. To many women's surprise, the

FSLN once again decided to appoint the organization's secretary general. It named Commander Doris Tijerino, someone with a long experience of struggle and a rather traditional (or nonfeminist) view of woman's role, previously the country's National Chief of Police."[8] This, coupled with the political disarticulation suffered throughout the Sandinista movement as a result of losing the 1990 elections, set the stage for the current situation in which revolutionary women began organizing outside as well as within AMNLAE.

When I lived in Managua during the early and mid-1980s, the people's revolution was exuberant. There were problems, of course, and the Sandinistas were beginning to feel the stranglehold of low intensity warfare: that catch-all term for all the different ways in which a succession of U. S. administrations tried to destabilize and destroy Nicaragua's radical option for change.

No need to go into great detail here, but I will briefly retrace some of the main points. As the Sandinista government launched programs in literacy and preventive medicine, as women's issues were addressed publicly for the first time in modern history, as the culture of the Atlantic coast was acknowledged and promoted, as land was distributed among those who worked it and new laws benefited working people, as poetry workshops sprang up throughout the country and jubilant murals appeared on the walls in streets that were once too dangerous for human survival, Reagan and then Bush tightened the noose.

The U.S. government couldn't tolerate what it called "another communist government" so close to home. Particularly threatening, I think, was a situation in which Marxists and Christians were working together toward what they both called *God's kingdom on earth*. The contras (dubbed "freedom fighters" by Reagan) were funded overtly and then covertly. When even that massive expenditure of U.S. taxpayers' money couldn't sustain an army lacking in popular support, the Bush administration forced the Sandinistas to hold elections. It helped forge an opposition coalition and pumped millions of dollars into a U.S.-style campaign.[9]

In February 1990, 55 percent of Nicaraguan voters, exhausted from war and an untenable economic situation, elected the UNO, a political coalition whose new government they believed the United States would support with generous economic aid. The FSLN, still the largest and most cohesive force in the country, winning 41 percent of the vote as a single party, was voted out of power. At this writing it's been two years since that dramatic revolutionary loss. The Sandinistas abided by their promise to respect the outcome of the elections, and peaceably turn the government over to the flimsy coalition that began to fall apart even before it took office. Still organized and powerful, the FSLN has been able to exert considerable political influence. For the first time in history, following a defeat at the polls, a revolutionary party has retained control of the army and police, and its elected representatives to the Council of State have been able to defend some important revolutionary gains. Under the circumstances, no small achievement.

As Dora María Téllez told me when I spoke with her in October 1991:

> More egalitarian property relations and the army: these have been our essential gains. Other political organizations might have launched the other admittedly important programs— health, education, and the rest—just as we did. Other political organizations *have*. But the changes we made in property relations, and the fact that the army is a people's force, these have been our unique contributions. Under the dictatorship no one was safe. Today, even after the FSLN's electoral loss, people can walk the streets without fearing for their lives. We need to protect these achievements.

Much has been destroyed. Land has been returned to the previous large landowners. Banks and important industries have been privatized once more. Foreign investment is being encouraged, and aspects of national sovereignty are slipping away. The Bush administration, the CIA, the U.S. embassy, and the local Catholic hierarchy now have more to say about what happens in Nicaragua than the democratically elected people's representatives do. Public education has become more conservative, with sex education eliminated. The possibilities for female advancement have also been curtailed. Most programs in public health are at a standstill.

Managua's streets have undergone profound change. The wonderful murals are gone. All those imprints in vibrant color that spoke of a people's history and liberation have been painted a flat gray. The names of streets and parks, which once honored revolutionary heroes and events, are being changed to more traditional names of politicians and saints. U.S. business ventures, such as Domino's Pizza and Continental Airlines, are more in evidence.

None of the millions promised by the United States should UNO win the elections have really benefited the Nicaraguan people. Most of those millions have not even materialized. Headlines blare frequent and multiple hospital deaths for lack of the most common medications, such as antibiotics and painkillers. The markets are filled with foods that most are too poor to buy. (Under the Sandinistas there were shortages and rationing, but everyone's basic needs were met by a subsidized monthly assortment of rice, beans, sugar, and other essentials.) And in the capital there are further signs of change. The city roars with the dull sound of late-model cars whose drivers arrogantly rev their motors through narrow cobblestone streets. These are the "Miamis," returned from their self-imposed exile in Florida and points north. They play their radios loud, which adds to the new noise level. They wear Nike shoes and ostentatious clothes and act as if they own the world. Dozens of young prostitutes line the streets in the center of Managua.

Nicaragua and its revolution are extraordinarily important in my life. When I returned to Managua to attend the solidarity conference about which I've already written, I knew I would be going back to find the shell of a dream that has been broken by internal error as well as by the belligerent hegemony of a "new world order." Already deeply immersed in my questions about socialism and feminism, I particularly wanted to talk to women. And that's exactly what I did—during almost every waking moment.

I found that my Nicaraguan sisters were seriously confronting the problems they articulated during ten years of revolution and a year and a half of conservative government. A realignment of forces in the wake of so many shattered projects has also enlarged the space for new priorities. AMNLAE went through periods of strength, problems, reassessment, and some degree of diminished energies. Once *the* revolutionary women's organization, it is now being challenged by other groups of women who do not feel represented in AMNLAE because of its lack of autonomy and its failure to take on a number of specifically feminist issues.

During and after the October conference, I talked to as many women as I could: members of AMNLAE (including some who worked in regions outside the capital), women's representatives in the union movement, women who considered themselves Sandinistas but felt uncomfortable with AMNLAE's program, and lesbian women who have emerged as part of a newly active gay, lesbian, and bisexual movement. I met with independent women working on projects that addressed gender-specific issues such as health and sex education, those active in women's centers that have split off from AMNLAE, and representatives of a loose movement of young women that calls itself The 52% Majority.

All these women are progressive. Most call themselves Sandinista. Many took an active part in the struggle to oust Somoza.[10] All agree that the decade of Sandinista government opened a vast economic, social, political, and cultural space for women, empowering them with a strong sense of their personal and collective identities. In no previous victorious revolution have women played such an essential role as in the Nicaraguan struggle. Many also believe that as the new government fought to survive, "women's issues" were relegated to a secondary place. Now they are beginning to think in more profoundly feminist terms.

These women also understand class struggle. This is important, because women becoming conscious of our womanness don't always have the kind of history or experience that enables us to view society with a class perspective. But these Nicaraguan women have been active militarily as well as politically in a successful revolutionary process, and continue to fight to expand the space gained during the years the FSLN was in power. One of the lesbian sisters told me: "We are sometimes surprised when we attend feminist meetings, for example at the regional or continental level. Many of the women address gender-specific issues outside the context of class. For us the two are inseparable. We are also surprised when we find lesbians in other places acting separately from gay men. We tend to work together."

I ached as I remembered my own experience during two decades of revolutionary involvement. I've often reflected upon how infrequently women of my generation, particularly in the places in which I lived, really examined our own lives with regard to our more "personal" aspects: sexuality, spirituality, memory. We were led to believe that it was "petty bourgeois" to pay too much attention to such "elitist" concerns.

Additionally, in my youth and young adulthood, problems such as compulsions, addictions, eating disorders and other evidence of abuse were seen as matters of will power. Try harder was the directive; push memory further and further down, was how it translated into our attitudes and behavior. An incipient consciousness existed, at least of the symptoms, but we didn't make the necessary connections between those symptoms and the underlying problems they signaled.

We always *said* that the personal is political (and even broke with the older left over this conviction), but to put the idea into practice proved much more difficult. The superhuman effort required to survive when people are forced to confront an enemy so much more powerful than they, produced a situation in which there was rarely time for reflection. One result of this inability to clearly see how male mechanisms clouded our perceptions was our acceptance of male privilege—even in some of its grossest manifestations—*as if it had nothing to do with an ongoing analysis of social change.*

A male leader, in his private life, might frequently use and abuse a succession of young women. As individual women we might refuse to participate, keep *ourselves* off the firing range. Or we might not. But the important thing is that this leader's behavior was never collectively challenged—*we did not challenge it*—as having anything to do with a man's vision or decision-making abilities. This unresolved contradiction is still painfully evident in Cuba, in Nicaragua, and I am sure in most other parts of the world.

When I try to understand why we were able to speak so eloquently about the personal being political—even to incorporate important elements of that concept into our lives, yet unable to push the perception further than we did—I inevitably come back to the mind/body split, something we did not articulate, much less pay attention to, back then. Among several generations of progressive people, Wilhelm Reich's theories had come and gone, and Reich's important early work was over-shadowed by what were widely considered the rantings of his later years. Alice Miller had not yet published her ground-breaking treatises linking childhood abuse and adult creativity. Feminist theory and therapy had not yet entered our lives.[11]

In the United States, we women who came to a left political consciousness in the 1960s and 1970s—in the context of the civil rights struggle and Vietnam—distinguished ourselves from the revolutionaries of preceding generations by honoring our personal perceptions and paying attention to our feelings. This led many women to struggle for equality within mixed organizations and, when that struggle failed, to break away to form organizations of our own. And so the second wave of feminism was born.

References to the second wave of feminism, useful perhaps in an ordering of history, may unfortunately bolster the erroneous idea that feminism belongs to the white, the industrialized, the women of the "first" world. We need to remember women's energy and leadership in the slave revolts, women who moved from the abolitionist cause to a struggle that also sought women's rights, immigrant women in the sweatshops fighting as workers *and as women.*

When I speak publicly about the failure of revolution to embrace a feminist agenda, some in the audience assume I am speaking about those strains of feminism that have emerged among mostly white women of privileged backgrounds, academics and other intellectuals from the United States and western Europe. I am not. I believe we have a great deal to give to one another, but that each culture, each history, produces its own feminist movement. It is precisely these *indigenous* movements that socialism fears.

For women who have remained in mixed political parties, or for women like myself whose arena of struggle has shifted to another country—where women fight to do battle side by side with men—feminist concerns, if acknowledged at all, are way down on the list of those issues we express in our discourse *or* our action. We are tough. We are disciplined. We don't think about how numb our bodies sometimes feel or how much we cannot remember. We don't stop to ask why. We don't know that looking for the answers to these new and complicated questions can have anything to do with how well we learn to know ourselves, fight our battles, and help sow the seeds of a system capable of addressing the needs of *all* human beings.

I wouldn't trade a single one of my years of revolutionary participation. But when I left Latin America and returned to the United States in 1984, I was suddenly and painfully confronted by my womanness: newly remembered childhood sexual abuse, reclaimed memory as a prerequisite to reconnecting mind and body, the challenge of trusting my deepest instincts, questions of sexuality, criticism, creativity. Less than a year after I returned home, I came out as a lesbian; I was forty-nine. The lessons learned from my need to separate and even repress the different parts of myself had been costly ones indeed.

On my return to Nicaragua in 1991, the women I met and spoke with were also questioning why feminism in its broadest definition—addressing power relations in gender, class, race and cultural configurations—was not allowed to consolidate and grow during the years of revolutionary government. Indeed, the revolution's mostly male leaders remained fearful of feminist ideas and incapable of coming to a positive consensus about the need for a feminist agenda.

Of course, the pressures exerted upon this process by U.S. "low intensity warfare," on the one hand, and counterrevolution and economic crisis inside the country, on the other, made it easier for the men in control to surrender to inertia or to what they so frequently refer to as their "natural impulses." And so they easily relegated feminism to a place of lesser importance. Now women feel that if they had taken a stronger stand on feminist issues, they would have helped to create a more secure foundation—perhaps one capable of resisting the external and internal pressures that voted it out of power. Now they speak out about abortion rights, violence against women, homophobia and heterosexism, the need for nonsexist sex education, and the importance of an autonomous women's movement. The last issue has the most important implications, since it is likely that women making their own organizational and programmatic decisions, rather than taking orders from a male-dominated party, would, indeed, address feminist concerns.

Some women have remained in AMNLAE. Some have moved into other areas of feminist struggle. The movement of young women that calls itself The 52% Majority, and the lesbian contingent particularly, are currently gaining in strength and numbers.

March 8, 9, and 10, 1991, marked the public debut of The 52% Majority. Issuing an invitation to "all nongovernmental women's organizations . . . women from the countryside and the city, from the Pacific and Atlantic coasts, women of all ages, religious beliefs, and political views," the organizers brought hundreds of unaffiliated women, along with members of AMNLAE who had grown dissatisfied with the organization, together at one of Managua's popular recreational spots.[12] This led to a bitter public exchange of accusatory letters, principally from the AMNLAE women who claimed that The 52% Majority was trying to divide their organization. Once again, instead of looking at the issues, women seemed to be hiding behind the proverbial smokescreen that protects the concept of unity at any cost rather than risk dealing with difficult questions.

AMNLAE expressed itself in an article published in *El Nuevo Diario,* an independent Managua daily sympathetic to the Sandinistas.[13] Under the subtitle "They Are Trying to Divide the Movement," a group of women from among the AMNLAE national leadership was quoted: "We are not against any feminine[sic] organization and we aren't here to take anything away from anyone, but neither are we going to stand for a group of women projecting themselves publicly at the expense of AMNLAE."

The article went on to explain that the AMNLAE women had been asked specifically about The 52% Majority, as some organizers of the new structure had been AMNLAE cadre during the period of Sandinista government. After describing the new group as "coming out for free love and a ferocious defense of lesbianism," the journalist added that it "also takes a radical position on conjugal relations, since the first thing it advises a couple with problems to do is to get a divorce." It hurts to see these women, who have so consistently struggled for equality and justice, engage in this sort of pettiness and echo such a conservative concept of womanhood and the family.

The interview's other line of attack was found in the

AMNLAE leaders' accusations concerning class. "The 52% Majority is an elite organization," they wrote. "It is made up of intellectuals, professionals, women whose standard of living and interests have nothing in common with those of the great majority who belong to AMNLAE." In their desire to avoid the impression that AMNLAE had suffered division, these women were implying that the issues addressed by the newer movement were not shared by most Nicaraguan women. "AMNLAE has survived," they said in the interview, "because it represents the interests of working women, women in the markets . . . pure *pueblo*." And when the reporter ended by asking them specifically what they thought of lesbianism, they responded to the question in chorus: "What lesbianism? Why we *love* men!"

Although datelined the following day, a response appeared in the same paper four days after the original interview.[14] Luz Marina Tórrez, Bertha Inés Cabrales, and Nora Meneses, who signed the public letter, began by making it clear that the women's centers they represented were frequented by housewives, market women, owners of small businesses, students, working women, and professionals "linked by the problems common to our gender." They conceded that these centers were, in effect, once affiliated with AMNLAE but had "separated themselves because they were critical of the organization's top-down style of operation and its emphasis on work that reproduces women's subordinate role in the family, daily life, and the political arena."

The letter went on to say that the three centers were

founded and maintained entirely through the work of local women. Then they listed their projects: an ongoing campaign around violence against women (rape, incest, battery, blackmail—interesting, this last category of abuse: a direct translation of what we call harassment), reproductive rights and women's health care, and con- sciousness-raising with men who have been judged re- miss in child support cases. They also mentioned their close work with union and professional organizations to train women in the nontraditional trades, as elec- tricians, solderers, and mechanics, as well as organize classes in the more historically female occupations of dressmaking, typing, and hairdressing.

In closing, the women wrote of the work the centers do to promote relations of equality and solidarity within the family, expressed in an equitable distribution of household tasks and provide sex education and family planning. "This is what we do. We ask the national leadership of AMNLAE: is this 'a dangerous campaign'? Are these not the concerns and most deeply felt needs of women everywhere? Is this work of ours really a danger to the unity of the women's movement?"

Several days later the debate again received more publicity.[15] Nineteen organizations and individual wo- men signed another public letter. The range was par- ticularly interesting; among the signatories were CEPRI's Program for Disabled Women, the women's secretariats of both the banana and cotton pickers, the Feminist Lesbian Group, foundations, feminist publishing houses, and popular education projects. Not only questioning the statements that the original article attributed to AMNLAE but also the professionalism of a newspaper that "should have checked its facts before publishing," the undersigned wrote that "as far as we know there is no such thing as a movement called 52%. Therefore, there are no centers, statements, nor common positions on the subjects of free love, lesbianism, conjugal relations, or irresponsible paternity. "There are," this letter went on, "women's groups, collectives and institutions that last March 8th took part in a public activity called The Festival of the 52%. All nongovernmental women's organizations were invited. . . . There is no orchestrated campaign against AMNLAE," the letter writers insisted, "but simply differences of opinion . . . legitimately explored in the context of a respect for freedom of expression, the rights of the individual, and those guarantees protecting free association."

These women and institutions ended by reiterating their "support for all those who work to defend the interests of Nicaraguan women, regardless of their political affiliation, if they have one." And they urged AMNLAE to assume an attitude of respect for difference, "be it political, generational, ethnic, of sexual preference, or work style." This openness on the part of women who came of age in a context of revolutionary struggle typifies women concerned with a feminist agenda—at least in the urban centers.

In January 1992, Nicaraguan women's commitment to a feminist vision exploded at a national conference in Managua. The organizers say they expected three hundred; more than eight hundred showed up. Women attending reported that they "took part in the conference out of a commitment to building an independent women's movement, not because they were sent as hand-picked representatives of trade unions or party-based women's organizations."[16] Milú Vargas, a well-known revolutionary lawyer and feminist, pointed out that this was "the first time the initiative [came] from the grassroots up." Once again, AMNLAE and the women's groups from some of the Sandinista trade unions were unwilling to stay involved throughout the planning process, although individual members of AMNLAE did remain part of the event.

Lesbian feminist groups were also present; as was Azucena Ferréy, a conservative and the only woman to serve on the contra's political directorate during the recent civil war. Martha María Blandón, one of the conference organizers, noted that "a self-selected group of feminists registered for the meeting. Most right-wing women do not identify with the women's movement," she said, but organizers felt they achieved their goal of "unity in diversity." Participants ranged from a peasant midwife who had never before visited the capital city, to feminist theoreticians, teachers, health workers, students, housewives, and trade unionists. Central on the meeting's agenda were the issues of health care and reproductive rights, education, sexuality, violence against women, political organizing, economic policy, and the environment.

The final declaration to emerge from this Nicaraguan

women's meeting "For Unity in Diversity" spoke to a qualitatively new perspective on women in society:

> The planning and execution of this meeting marks the begin-
> ning of *a new political culture*. We want to find our own
> definition of power and how to exercise it, in order to improve
> upon those male forms which we have internalized and re-
> produced. It is in this sense that we recognize the self-con-
> voking, autonomous and pluralist character of our effort, ex-
> pression of a common need, and *a democratic way of building
> solidarity among women*
>
> [ . . .] *Our gender rights are the political rights of citizens. A
> democracy that does not recognize us as protagonists of our
> own lives, is not a democracy.*[17]

At the end of March 1992, under the banner "A New Woman, A New Power," some five hundred Central American women took part in the first regional feminist conference, hosted by Nicaraguan feminists at the exclusive tourist resort of Montelimar.[18] Motherhood, domestic violence, abortion, lesbianism, prostitution and women's leadership were some of the topics discussed by delegates from various grassroots, feminist, indigenous, and peasant organizations. Lesbian and religious groups were represented, along with displaced persons and war refugees. A number of delegates claimed that little progress was made in previous years due to the war and to the prejudices of both the left and right. Many felt the forum gave them a first real opportunity to debate feminist thought in Latin America. Isabel Ascencio, a Salvadoran lay worker with *Paz y*

*Concertacion*, told the press: "During these years, some of us have devoted all our energies to the political struggle. Now we need to recognize and take up the liberating elements of feminism."

A few days after the forum of Central American feminists, AMNLAE held its fifth national assembly; about four hundred delegates attended. Gladys Báez, in her report to those participating, highlighted the work carried out in the organization's forty-eight women's houses. In the current economically and politically hostile environment, these centers continue to offer women medical and legal services, technical training, and gender workshops.[19]

A lesbian, gay, and bisexual movement emerged in Nicaragua in 1985. On one hot rainy October night I talked to several of the women involved. They told me that at first they had simply been a group of friends who happened to live in the same neighborhood, noticed one another, and began getting together, "just to talk about the issues people had: relationships, problems with our families, that sort of thing."[20] Most of the young women and men were active in the FSLN, some as members, others as sympathizers. Toward the end of 1986 they began to organize more formally and a larger network emerged, with perhaps some fifty people in all.

The Victoria Mercado Brigade appeared on the scene a couple of years earlier.[21] It was made up of lesbians and gay men from San Francisco who had come down to do construction work in solidarity with the people of Nicaragua. It is clear that there has been a good deal of reciprocal influence between both countries' gay movements in the context of our very different cultures and historical moments.

The Nicaraguan lesbians even briefly considered trying to get AMNLAE involved in their organizing efforts, but desisted. They talked about whether they wanted to focus on sexual orientation as a feminist issue or as one that affects women in general (whether or not they are feminists), if they wanted to make a public presence—in short, what kind of work they wanted to be doing. The initial decision was to begin by doing consciousness raising among themselves.

Lesbians and gays who were closeted, even if their sexual orientations were known, had generally been respected within the FSLN. But in mid-1988 a number of those who had been organizing and becoming more public about their sexual orientation were summoned to the Office of State Security. They were told that by getting together as they'd been doing they were jeopardizing their party membership. There was no detention or physical mistreatment, but the interrogations involved a morbid curiosity about gay life as well as a general lack of respect for the individuals called in, and resulted in the kind of coercion that is particularly difficult for a person who is being told she or he must choose between revolutionary affiliation and openly addressing their sexual identity.

This repressive measure hurt the movement and undoubtedly forced many *out* homosexuals back into the closet. Most, in the midst of war, opted to continue in the FSLN and silence that other part of themselves: a painful choice. About a year later, Dora María Téllez, then Minister of Public Health, recruited some of these same young people to join innovative brigades doing AIDS education work. The invitation provoked a confrontation between the office of State Security and the Minister of Public Health that ended up validating the group's prior organizational efforts. This brought a certain legitimacy to the gay community, which grew stronger while the FSLN was in power.

One of the women described the original group's first public appearance. It was at the Sandinista revolution's tenth anniversary parade. About fifty lesbians and gay men lined up where the national directorate would be sure to see them when they marched by. "We all went out wearing our black T-shirts with the pink triangles, men and women together. It was our way of telling the FSLN that after ten years of struggle we were there, we were Sandinistas and we were with them . . ." She noted the varied reactions of the FSLN leaders: "Some laughed, some remained serious, no one really said anything. But for us it was important. It was our collective coming out, you might say."

On July 30, 1991, Gay Pride was celebrated publicly in Managua for the first time.[22] In commemoration of the fourth anniversary of the The Office of State Security's repressive measure against them, more than two hundred lesbians, gays, and bisexuals hosted an evening at Coro de Angeles, one of the city's most popular clubs. They invited the press, featured the film *Torch Song Tril-*

*ogy,* as well as local cultural numbers, and opened a broad discussion aimed at responding to the questions society, and homosexuals themselves, might have about gay people's lifestyles, needs, and options. Many non-gay friends accompanied the community on that occasion, and press coverage was extremely positive.[23]

This event inaugurated the Movement of Nicaraguan Lesbian Feminists and Homosexuals.[24] It's interesting, especially when we consider how many different political tendencies exist among lesbians in the United States, that the Nicaraguan movement calls itself "Lesbian Feminist." In obvious and not so obvious ways, I believe that the Sandinista Revolution, in spite of its homophobia, opened a political space where feminism could begin to breathe.

The personal stories I heard that night in October are not that different from our own: the familiar early questioning of sexual identity, decisions about coming out at work or in the community, discrimination from most quarters, understanding from a few, the never-ending struggle for dignity and a sense of self-worth. These Nicaraguan lesbians also told some stories that were unique. Two were particularly interesting to a discussion of heterosexism, homophobia, and revolutionary change in Nicaragua.

Hazel elicited a round of nods and smiles when she said she was from Matagalpa. For some reason, the north-central city, historically deeply Catholic, seems to be home to a large number of out lesbians. Like many young women exploring their sexuality, Hazel began by assuming she was heterosexual and then considered herself bisexual, when she began having problems with her political militancy. Bisexuality was seen as a political deviancy by her immediate superiors in the FSLN. "But my history is an interesting one," she continued, "because I made a trip to Cuba about then. And you could say that's where I really began to accept myself as a lesbian.

"It's contradictory," Hazel admitted, "because Cuba is a country where homosexuality has been severely persecuted. Still, I grew a lot there. I began going around with other lesbians and gay men. Before that, in Nicaragua, even though I was in a relationship with a woman, I never really had a community. In Cuba I found a *massive* community." Hazel went on to describe "an enormous parallel world" with clubs where an un-advertised but clearly gay culture exists. On a second trip to Cuba she studied at the Latin American Film School.[25] She said:

> In the world of artists, well [homosexuality] is even more accepted. I met students from all over Latin America, from Africa and Asia, and I got to know much more about lesbian and gay culture, what was happening on other continents, I met a lot more people. That's when I *really* came out. I learned to live my lesbianism much more completely. At school there were no prejudices at all. We had complete freedom to do whatever we wanted, live together, whatever . . .

I lived in Cuba when homosexuality was repressed as well as during the years when it began, with dif-ficulty, to claim a very small space. It does not surprise me that Hazel found a flowering gay culture in Havana nor that an official government institution made room for and encouraged respect for sexual difference. Cuba's socialist revolution is one of the few such experiments still alive and—with all its failings—perhaps the healthiest. I would be the last, however, to say that life for gay women and men in Cuba is easy. An old friend in Havana, a lesbian who has made a satisfying life and is highly respected in intellectual circles, recently sent me a letter in which she spoke about herself but refrained from using precise language when describing her life style. I will go into more detail later on about feminism and socialism in Cuba. Here I would just like to say I believe that when socialism is honestly dedicated to making a better life for everyone, heterosexism and homophobia, too, must begin to erode; if it does not, the experiment will fail. In Cuba, as elsewhere, the erosion has a long way to go. But the process is under way.

Another story by Mary has particular relevance here and seems to contradict some aspects of Hazel's experience as well as the history of repression against that group of gay women and men who began organizing in Managua in the mid-1980s. As with all relationships, the one between the FSLN as a political party and its homosexual members has had its complexities and contradictions. Mary insisted that "inside the FSLN it hasn't only been repression . . . my experience hasn't been anything like what you've been talking about," she told Hazel and the rest of us.

Mary said she was a long-time member of the party and that her comrades had always known that she was a lesbian. "No one's ever accused me of anything, and no one's ever failed to offer me positions of responsibility because of my sexuality." She recalled a meeting of the Sandinista Assembly at which it was explicitly stated that no reprisals should be taken against anyone because of his or her sexual preference. "I'm not saying that this policy has always been carried out," she admitted, ". . . it's depended a lot on who happens to be in charge, on what kind of a human being that person is, the breadth, the vision."

Nevertheless, Mary insisted that this attitude of acceptance was "something that's made an impression on comrades from other places." She said that—like some other aspects of women's role within the Sandinista Revolution, or the fact that Christians and Marxists work toward the same political goals—it's "something that the movement here in Nicaragua has given to the rest of Latin America. It's made others stop and think about the fact that homosexuals can be revolutionaries, it's a small contribution we've made." And, referring to a comment by another women about how the Nicaraguan revolutionary context avoided the ghettoization of gays, Mary added that: ". . . not creating ghettos really is important. We need to defend our place in society as a whole and make society respect us for what we are, for what we do, for our work."

All the lesbian women I talked with were actively involved in revolutionary projects. One is a doctor;

several work in public health. One edits a feminist publication. Another is involved in popular sex education. The conversation moved on to sexism within the gay movement—*machismo* as it affects all women, not just lesbians—the opening of a couple of gay clubs in Managua, how far women in the countryside are from a discussion of any of these issues, and the reassessment of attitudes towards homosexuality that is part of the FSLN's general reexamination of all aspects of struggle.[26]

Nicaragua has a number of conservative women's organizations, some linked to right or centrist political parties, others religious or social in origin. Their programs are those traditional to such groups. Women are seen as subservient mainstays of the nuclear family, a support system for patriarchy and capitalism. I will not discuss these organizations here because they have nothing to do with feminism— except insofar as they are expressions of the patriarchical fear of feminist ideology and support the status quo in the promotional work they do among bourgeois and/or dependent women.

At this point there is obvious tension among the different sectors of the revolutionary women's movement in Nicaragua. I believe that the various tendencies will eventually come together around specific issues— violence against women, abortion, and others—and that building a coalition will break down some of the barriers. After all, these women share a common history in a country where struggle has been particularly intense, and change compressed into a dramatically short period of time. Yet AMNLAE, with its extraordinary history of struggle, still shows itself to be antagonistic to lesbians and other outspoken feminists. In popular discourse, the very words *feminist* and *lesbian* are often used as epithets for women who are accused of being "too radical."

I think about Nicaragua under the Sandinistas. In spite of the way it was (mis)represented in the U.S. press, it was never a purely socialist experiment. The Sandinistas combined what they considered the most useful of a number of ideological frameworks: socialism, Christianity, and the ideas of Augusto C. Sandino, the revolutionary Nicaraguan peasant leader from the 1920s and 1930s after whom their movement is named. A mixed economy and political pluralism have always been important parts of the project.

Developing when it did, as the second wave of feminism emerged in the industrialized nations, the pre-victory Sandinista movement attracted a large number of women to its ranks.[27] More importantly, many of these women had feminist concerns and struggled with their brothers-in-arms around issues such as women in leadership, traditional social mores that inhibit women's participation, and the need to address these issues *during*, and not after, the revolutionary war.

When victory came, approximately one-third of the Sandinista army was female. Women were military commanders: Dora María Téllez led the liberation of León, the country's first free territory; another woman commander, Mónica Baltodano, helped lead the tactical retreat of several thousands from Managua to Masaya at the very end of the war. Nora Astorga was the special attorney general in charge of handling the trials of Somoza's torturers and henchmen. Later she headed the Nicaraguan delegation to the United Nations during the last difficult years of contra war. These are only several of many examples. From the beginnings of peace-time reconstruction, women have held positions of political power and leadership. Several were ministers and vice ministers of state. A few rose within the ranks of the party, and quite a few held seats in the National Assembly.

But peace wasn't to last. And as death was once more thrust upon the land, feminist and other issues that the traditionalists considered of secondary importance were pushed aside. The U.S. government, through a series of open and covert actions, had begun its efforts to undermine the Nicaraguan revolution even before the Sandinistas won the war. In a poor agricultural country whose last two harvests had been devastated by fighting, there was little time to devote to realizing the "more subtle" dreams. The need to organize a defense against the contra aggression became the priority.

During their ten years in power, in spite of a tremendous struggle for survival, the Sandinistas did manage to change women's lives considerably. One of the new government's earliest decrees prohibited using images of the female body in commercial advertising. Special health programs were designed to meet the needs of women and children. Domestic servants, most of them female, were encouraged to organize for job security, benefits, and a ten-hour day. The Women's Offices were established to attend to legal problems.

Nicaragua always has had a high rate of what they call paternal irresponsibility, men who father children by several women and then move on, leaving the mothers to support themselves and their offspring. Through the Women's Offices single mothers could now demand child support, and where possible the father's salary was attached. Some sewing cooperatives were set up for women in prostitution, to help them learn other marketable skills if they wanted to get out of the life.

As the war and economic crisis intensified, many of these projects were abandoned. And of course the loss of the 1990 elections deeply affected women's gains. Ironically, many mothers, strained to the limit by an intolerable economic situation and a war that was killing their children, were among those who voted against the Sandinistas. They held to the hope that UNO's promise of food on the table and sons and daughters home from the battlefield might be fulfilled by a government looked upon favorably by the United States.

But what has happened, for women and for others, in the year since that election? According to the National Workers' Front (FNT), the new economic plan has forced more than 13,000 women farm workers, 3,000 women factory workers, and 2,000 women health workers into the ranks of the unemployed. It is estimated that almost 70 percent of all women workers in Nicaragua are heads of households, and that more than half of these are single mothers, with an average of four to six children. These women must rely exclusively on their wages, which average $50 a month. The essential basket of minimal necessary foodstuffs currently costs $160 a month.[28]

The first year of the Chamorro government did not improve life for Nicaraguans, but instead condemned tens of thousands to even greater poverty. Now *sobrevivencia* (survival) is the word most often heard. The astounding relative equality achieved by the Sandinistas for female and male farm workers quickly faded; women, of course, were traditionally the first fired from all job categories. Other changes have been particularly cruel to women in the countryside. Of the seventy Rural Infant Service Centers (clinics) established during the Sandinista government, only ten still offer a few scant services. Yet women are still organizing, this time with the conviction that gender-specific demands must not be sacrificed in favor of broader political concerns.

Might more courageous attention to a feminist agenda in Nicaragua have made a difference to the survival of the Sandinista process? Could it have changed the quality of life for women who are, after all, more than half of every population? Would they still have been taken in by the lies of the UNO campaign? Would a feminist agenda have made the revolution stronger? And what about Cuba, the Soviet Union, the countries of Eastern Europe, Vietnam? Had there not been such an aversion to a specifically feminist agenda in each of these countries, might socialism have been strengthened? These are questions that can no longer wait for answers.

In Nicaragua, women participated in the Sandinista struggle in numbers vastly greater than anything we've known throughout the history of revolutions.[29] And, as we've seen, the Sandinista Revolution *did* do a great deal to change women's lives. But many Nicaraguan feminists believe that not enough was done, that issues such as abortion (in spite of the Catholic hierarchy's opposition), violence against women, or the mobilization of women around other gender-specific concerns, should have been pushed harder. I agree.

It has been pointed out that there are at least three main sectors of Nicaraguan society that eventually acted out against the very revolution that gave them the most benefits: peasants, indigenous peoples, and women. Today contra peasants are demanding of the UNO government the very things the Sandinistas offered them (land, technical assistance, credit). Why are contra and Sandinista peasants only now joining together to struggle for their common interests? The war they waged against one another cost more than 30,000 lives. Could it be that some peasants became contras because they were not at the center of the policies affecting their lives?

At the Second Symposium on Autonomy, held in November 1991, Sandinista and non-Sandinista (Yatama and other) indigenous peoples recognized that the Autonomy Law, created and supported by the Sandinista government in cooperation with the people themselves, laid the only solid, legal basis for the present-day struggles against UNO's virtual abandonment of the Atlantic coast. Through the autonomy process the Sandinistas did correct past errors, but perhaps too late not to have paid a serious price.

And women? War and economic crisis aside, despite the tremendous benefits and positive changes the decade of Sandinista administration made in women's lives, this sector—as I've noted—helped vote in a government that would try to reverse all of their hard-won gains. Again, I believe it is a matter of subject vs. object. Had women truly been empowered, would they have abandoned the revolution?

Something that happened after the Sandinistas were voted out of power speaks of what was surely a timid approach to a feminist agenda, even within a party that thinks of itself as the vanguard. At the FSLN's first congress, held in July 1991, a considerable number of delegates wanted Dora María Téllez on the national directorate. I alluded to this earlier. Two places had been vacated for different reasons. There was discussion, but there also seems to have been considerable "ol' boy" politicking, and the panel remained exclusively male.

Unity and continuity were the arguments used in defense of reelecting the slate as a single entity; challenging the inadequacies or errors of particular directorate members, some felt, might weaken or divide the organization. The new elected members were certainly worthy. But in my opinion and that of others it was time to reflect more accurately the reality of the Sandinista struggle by including this extraordinary leader—who is also a woman and a feminist. How long must we listen to the phrase "for the sake of unity" as the justification for failing to deal with problems whose solutions threaten positions of power that rapidly become institutionalized or entrenched?

And how do we define unity? The Sandinista leadership's definition in this case—as in so many—translates as the continued acceptance of *unity among men*. Here again, the unity not to be threatened is the status quo. When will unity come to mean a power-sharing of all participants, a true representation of all parties?

There has been a great deal of discussion about this in Nicaragua. Téllez herself has stated that the inclusion of a single woman shouldn't be separated from the context of women's positions generally. Broader attention to women's issues throughout the ten years of Sandinista power would undoubtedly have helped raise consciousness. At a grassroots level, more work around women's roles in society is essential; more attention to developing a feminist agenda should have been a priority during the previous government, and it should be a priority now. The Sandinista leadership has promised to "make room for a woman" on the directorate to be elected at the next party congress. But again, it is not a matter of *men making room for a woman*. Our history shows us that women must claim and inhabit the room we need, the room that patriarchy has usurped through so many constricted lifetimes. Only an autonomous movement is capable of bringing this about.

I want to stop here and take another look at the issue of unity at all costs, of unity vs. the specter of division. No one can doubt that principled unity is essential, especially against a strong enemy. *Divide and conquer* has been used against every movement for change. But a plea for genuine unity cannot be allowed to become a cover-up for injustice. Think of how often the unity argument has been used to create an atmosphere where we pretend away the serious problems that plague our communities.

These are oppressed communities, and yes, their members need to support one another. But we never truly support one another when we become a party to injustice, when we turn our backs on violence and deceit—or are afraid to face our own failures. In such cases, the language of *unity at any cost* becomes a language of oppression.

We witnessed this in the black community when some of its finest women writers began to tell stories of incest and abuse. Some black men were angered at the telling of such stories. All black people, they said, are oppressed by the white power structure; they must stick together and certainly not wash their dirty laundry where others can see and use it against them. The idea that washing dirty laundry in public is somehow worse than the laundry's existence and that exposing it compounds the grief, or that "two wrongs do not make a right," are claims frequently used to silence those who dare to ask the questions, who challenge, who accuse. And inevitably the silencing becomes a new language of oppression. Victims of sexual and other abuse know this language well. It is used by the perpetrator to shame us into silence and—until very recently—was echoed by society. Only in the past decade have we begun to crack its armor.

Again and again, unity at any cost is prescribed as a panacea. How often, in a situation where a wife or a child has suffered severe family abuse, have social workers or the courts tried to keep the couple or the family together, even when such a dangerous under- standing of unity clearly threatens the abused person's safety and compromises her future? Unity for unity's sake is not always the preferable course: in a couple, in a family, in a community, or in a political movement.

Today many in the progressive Jewish community struggle with accusations of betrayal because they see their Palestinian sisters and brothers as human beings, joined at the root and deserving—as the Israelis are—of a home. *United at all costs* becomes a silencing, a way of oppressing others. And the core issues of anti-Semitism on the one hand and Zionism on the other are effective- ly obscured.

When we left mixed organizations to found or enter women-only groups, political women of my generation remember being accused of dividing the movement. In the mixed organizations we had been the ones to make the coffee, type the position papers, look after the children, care for and sleep with the male leaders—until one day we tired of being maidservants to men who spoke of a "new man" and a new society.

In all the socialist experiments there has been an emphasis on constructing a model human being: socially responsible, generous, internationalist, healthy in mind and body. But what is the message, if this new model is male, heterosexual, light skinned, and with conservative personal values? How well I remember children in Cuba, including my own, chanting "Seremos como el Che!" ("We will be like Che!").[30] If you could not be like this particular revolutionary hero, what strikes might you have against you before you even grew into your own unique personhood? How lacking in confidence might you feel?

In our various movements, only by regrouping out of our strength were we able to know ourselves, find our voices, and envision the kinds of changes worth doing battle for. Many of us have returned to the mixed struggle with much more to give. Others remain separate, still unable to trust those who continue to tell us to "wait until the time is right."

If recent events in the former Soviet Union, in Eastern Europe, and in Nicaragua teach us anything, it is that the old myths have been dismembered. Pretending away problems for the sake of some fragile and fictitious unity is an invitation to destruction rather than a safeguard to creating a just society. It is nothing more or less than denial.

# 3
# SOME HISTORY . . .

In those days, there was only one revolution
going, and though it viewed people as workers,
not men and women,
you signed its petitions,
sensing that freedom begets more freedom.

**—Enid Dame**[1]

L ong before my return to Nicaragua I, like so many others, thought about the international succession of popular losses in recent months and years: the U.S. invasions of Grenada and Panama, the apparent decline of socialism throughout Eastern Europe and in the Soviet Union, the Sandinista's electoral loss in Nicaragua, and the terrible threat that hangs over Cuba and North Korea.[2] Both the enormity and brutality of the U.S.-led massacre in the Persian Gulf and the broad appeal of its yellow-ribboned cheering section here at home speak profoundly about how far we have been manipulated into accepting a new world order, where the unchallenged might of a global military-industrial complex is acceptable national behavior.[3]

Although undermined and in many cases murdered outright by the United States and its allies, there is no doubt in my mind that the socialist experiments in the construction of a just and process-oriented society were clearly weakened by a range of internal problems. Socialism made mistakes—systemic as well as occasional—that contributed to its inability to remain in power.

As a feminist, I look not only at women's roles in the different experiments but at how these experiments grappled or refused to grapple with a feminist vision. One may begin by considering the ways in which these revolutions addressed or failed to address issues of women's equality. In all of them, some attention to "women's issues" was promised in initial programs and platforms. In some of the more recent revolutions—the Vietnamese and Nicaraguan, for example—many more than a few outstanding women participated in the struggle for power. A few women occupied important positions in the new peoples' governments and life for women invariably improved, especially during the first years.

But then something happened. In each case, to varying degrees and in different ways, depending upon the particular culture and moment in time, women's issues were pushed aside. For one thing, they were generally viewed as just that: *women's* issues, rather than as issues important to the whole of society. In periods of armed struggle, when every hand is needed against a force so much larger and more powerfully equipped, women and even children are welcomed into the trenches. When the war is won, however, men once again need women for something else: the solace and comforts of home, with someone pampering their daily needs, giving birth to and raising their children. When the dramatic necessities of guerrilla warfare give way to the longer term and more complex problems of government, men always limit women's space. What is more confusing and harder to deal with is the fact that many women are themselves willing to retreat into these more traditional roles.

On the other hand, changing consciousness requires profound changes in the nature of a country's educational effort: changes in the methods as well as in the content of education. Critical thinking must be encouraged. Everything must be questioned. Such a challenge to traditional patterns of thought, even to traditional *revolutionary* patterns of thought, is very difficult to come by. A feminist vision, in the broadest sense, is required.

Of course we must be careful to assess each revolutionary experience within its historic framework, not to expect more from a particular situation than its time can give. But this is always about power: who has it, what they will do to keep it, and what can be done by those who lack it so that it may be distributed more equitably. Where gender is concerned, this question has its particular contours, because women are not a minority. In fact, in every country we are slightly more than half the population, a condition that gives us great potential for struggle. A multiply oppressed group and the majority:

the combination would seem to be a sure recipe for rebellion. But patriarchy has developed around the ownership and inheritance of property, and so women become property of men in deference to the need to ensure the continuance of their line. Patriarchal societies, socialist as well as capitalist, push us to internalize our oppression.

For most of civilization and in most countries, women's sphere of influence—women's power—has been the home. Women's socialization goes back generations, indeed centuries, creating an atmosphere that many of us seem as unwilling to relinquish as men are to move into. We frequently hear a woman say, "Leave me alone! I *like* things the way they are," or "Come on . . . I *want* to be taken care of!" When we accept this as choice, what we fail to realize is that the woman who expresses herself in such a way is attempting to retain the only power she believes she has, power in the home sphere. But in capitalist patriarchy, this too turns out to be an illusion.[4]

In its goal to create a more egalitarian society, why has socialism found it so much easier to address class than gender—or, for that matter, race, sexuality, culture, spirituality, and other identity issues that have to do with cultural history and changing consciousness, as well as with the means and methods of production? I want to continue to explore the contradictions that arise when socialist and feminist agendas evolve together and then part ways, always favoring the former at the expense of the latter.

When we talk about revolution, we may be talking about a revolution in the means of production, how people's labor is organized and who profits from that labor. This is referred to as a revolution of the infrastructure, of the base. Or we may be talking about a revolution in human consciousness, the recognition of and respect for differences: the full personhood of women as well as men, people of diverse affectional or sexual orientation, those of different races or ethnicities, those with a range of belief systems, or abilities. If we are talking about a revolution that can last, that will touch everyone, that will be capable of giving the full measure of her or his identity to every person, we must be sure we are talking about all of these. Ultimately, people will only fight for a process they feel belongs to them.

Most of the social and political upheavals of this century—the Bolshevik and Chinese revolutions, those in Vietnam and Algeria, Cuba, Nicaragua, and others—came about proclaiming the need to change both people's consciousness *and* the base. They at least gave lip service to a respect for ethnic and cultural difference. Inspired by Marxist analysis, revolutionaries saw relations of production and a heightened consciousness as dialectically interrelated, inseparable. In the first socialist revolution, Lenin understood the relationship between superstructural change and a change in the means of production. The body of his work repeatedly warns against economism and elitism.

But the revolutionaries who followed distorted Marx's basic idea that those who produce must control the power and product of their labor. They also strayed from Lenin's guidelines. Lenin's theory of the party, *as interpreted by his followers*, focuses upon a vanguard group of men (and, eventually, why not: a few women might be included as long as they did not pose a threat to the male line) who would interpret the needs and capabilities of the workers. Lenin's idea of a vanguard included representatives of *all* the working sectors of society. "Leninists," however, were unable to avoid the emergence of vanguards that themselves would become elitist. Workers, including workers of color and women workers, were to control their labor and their lives. But in practice, that's not the way it worked out. Years of betrayal—working for change alongside men, only to find that the new society does not include or even represent us fully—illustrate how essential it is that women make the decisions that affect our lives; as essential as it is that as workers we control the fruits of our labor, or that indigenous peoples enjoy an autonomy that assures sacred traditions.

It's not just a matter of Lenin being "right," though, and his followers "wrong." This seems too easy an appraisal. Perhaps, in the light of feminist theory, Lenin's view of power, his concept of *taking power*, needs to be analyzed differently. Of course oppressed peoples must wrest power from their oppressors, but hasn't there been an over-focus on a male definition of power? Feminist theory is not the only discipline that redefines traditional concepts of power. Paulo Freire's work in the field of popular education tells us *empowerment* only comes when people learn from their own experience.[5] Liberation theology, as practiced in the Christian base communities throughout Latin America and elsewhere, has focussed more on people and their development than on seizing state power. (When you focus only on seizing it, you only need to deal with how to keep it, rather than with how to educate people to new notions of what it means.) Perhaps this is not simply about changing the relations of power, but about *empowering all people*.

Today's feminists also pay much closer attention than was paid in the 1920s and 1930s to the discrepancies so often evident between a man's stated ideology and the way he conducts his life. Without wishing to cast a shadow upon Lenin's great contribution to revolutionary thought and practice, I cannot help but wonder if Alexandra Kollontai's portrayal of Senya in *A Great Love* is, as many claim, a thinly disguised reference to Lenin himself.[6] If it is true that Lenin preached women's equality while subjecting revolutionary women to his sexual and emotional service, it is easier to understand how his vision of representation may also have been flawed. Today we have a deeper and more demanding understanding of the ways in which theory and practice move together, feeding one another.

Then there is the question of method. For those of us struggling in small progressive or revolutionary groups to change society against structures so much more powerful and sophisticated, it was clear that we needed organization, discipline, a functioning leadership. Political parties seemed to offer that, and for a long time we counted on them to come through for us. From time to time we might have questioned the discrepancies, but for years many of us justified the non-feminist direction of our struggle in the name of a mythologized future in which we would no longer be oppressed—not at all unlike the problem confronted by women within the major religions, insofar as the positions allotted them are concerned. In the evolution of Marxist revolution, Lenin's democratic centralism—with regard to women as well as to other groups—ended up imposing a rigorous centralism without a workable democracy.

When some women began to question the top-down and predominantly male hierarchies, we tended to create more horizontally organized collectives, capable of work styles based on consensus, greater fluidity between theory and practice, less defensiveness in questioning traditional social relations, and much more creative risk taking. We gave birth to extraordinary projects and reaped important lessons from some of these experiences. But unequal struggle and the highly competitive nature of our societies eventually proved too much for the survival of most nonhierarchical structures. It now seems clear to me that the Leninist conception of the party, as implemented by successive generations of revolutionaries, was one of the major factors impeding a feminist vision of revolution.

Trotsky wrote of this in *The Revolution Betrayed*. Alexandra Kollontai, Rosa Luxemburg, and Wilhelm Reich, among others, cautioned that authoritarianism would reproduce the very inequality the revolution was committed to eradicate. They warned of the dangers inherent in ignoring people's needs for spiritual, sexual, critical, and creative freedoms.[7] Revolutionaries have always struggled with the issue of how to strike the most procreative balance between changing the relations of production and changing human consciousness. But after a few months or years in power most of the revolutionary experiences did an about face or slacked off in their efforts to effect a radical change in people's consciousness. Faced with the enormous difficulties inherent in changing society, and besieged by a capitalist system fighting to maintain global hegemony, the revolution's tradition-bound leadership believed retreat was necessary in order to consolidate the all-important economic changes.

Throughout the history of revolutions, there have always been women who understood this problem. Raya Dunayevskaya, the young woman from the Ukraine who at the age of thirteen immigrated to the United States where she learned about struggle in the ghettos of Chicago, has given us a lifetime of thought and a body of work precisely about these issues. Dunayevskaya always asked questions. She was expelled from the U.S. Communist Party's youth group in 1928, joined the Trotskyites, and in 1937 became Trotsky's Russian-language secretary during his exile in Mexico. But two years later, at the time of the Hitler-Stalin Pact, she broke with him over a basic question of definition. Her study of the Russian economy and of

Marx's early writings convinced her that Russia was not socialist but state capitalist—and that state capitalism would in fact be a new world stage.

During the dark years of McCarthyism, Duna-yevskaya made a philosophical breakthrough that would further shape her understanding of society. In Hegel's Absolutes she saw a dual movement: from practice that is itself a form of theory and from theory reaching to philosophy. This led her first to a rereading of Marx's early work, and then to the discovery of his final writings (which she retranslated because she said the version published in Moscow was "marred by footnotes which flagrantly violate Marx's content and intent").[8]

Dunayevskaya called herself a Marxist Humanist. Marx's "thoroughgoing Naturalism or Humanism" informed her revolutionary participation, which in turn fueled her theory.[9] Throughout the 1960s, Duna-yevskaya participated in the movements for civil rights in the United States and for national liberation in other parts of the world. At the same time she was writing important treatises that linked her interpretation of Marx to issues of race and the struggles of colonized peoples. For her, women's liberation was an unnegoti-able concern.

Adrienne Rich, in her forward to a new edition of one of Dunayevskaya's most important texts, tells us how this revolutionary "grapples, in the face of the Stalinist legacy, with the question: *What happens after? . . .* What turns revolutionary leaders into tyrants?" Rich asks.[10] "Why did the Russian Revolution turn backward on itself? How do we make the 'continuing revolution,' 'the revolution in permanence' in which this cannot happen?"

Rich reminds us of Dunayevskaya's ability, almost absent among the mostly white male theorists whose thoughts bog down our canon, to respect and learn from

> . . . other kinds of thinking and other modes of expression: those of the Third World, of ordinary militant women, of working people. . . . Where Engels posited "the world historic defeat of the female sex,". . . Dunayevskaya notes that Marx saw the resistance of the women in every revolution, not simply how they were disempowered by the development of patriarchy and by European invasion and colonization.

Rich and Dunayevskaya show the absurdity of "the notion that Marx's Marxism means class struggle is primary or that racism and male supremacism will end when capitalism falls."[11]

In her 1981 introduction to *Rosa Luxemburg, Women's Liberation, and Marx's Philosophy of Revolution,* Dunayevskaya herself provides an excellent point of departure for those of us who seek answers in the multiple intersections of class, race, gender, and sexual orientation. She warns that

> the greatest contradiction in all these cross currents stems from the very depth of the economic political social crises, which produce a great desire for shortcuts to freedom. Instead of grappling with the working out of a philosophy of liberation for our age, theoreticians look only for "root causes" of oppression. This is good, but hardly good enough. It narrows the whole relationship between causality and freedom; it im-

pedes the dual rhythm of revolution that demands not only the overthrow of the old but the creation of the new. In place of hewing out a road to total freedom, it gets hemmed in by one form or another of economic determinism.

Dunayevskaya explains that

> Marx's last writings—the *Ethnological Notebooks*—are a critical determinant in themselves and in the light they cast on Marx's work as a totality, as he was completing the circle begun in 1844. With his study of works on primitive societies, like Morgan's *Ancient Society*, [he] was diving into the study of human development, both in different historic periods and in the most basic Man/Woman relationship. The concept he held fast was the one he had worked out in his *1844 Economic Philosophic Manuscripts*. This was not, as anthropologists would have it, simply a move from a philosophic to an empiric, scientific, and anthropological view. Rather, as a revolutionary, Marx's hostility to capitalism's colonialism was intensifying. The question was how total must be the uprooting of existing society and how new the relationship of theory to practice. [He saw] the possibility of new human relations, not as they might come through a mere "updating" of primitive communism's equality of the sexes, as among the Iroquois, but as [he] sensed they would burst forth from a new type of revolution.[12]

The similarity between this interpretation of Marx and questions being asked in feminist discourse is striking. Dunayevskaya goes on to say that not a single one of the post-Marx Marxists "worked on the ground Marx . . . laid out, either on precapitalist societies or on the question of Women's Liberation." This task has fallen to us, she claims, because "ours is an age that has witnessed a movement *from practice*, the emergence of a whole new third world—Afro-Asian, Latin American, Middle Eastern—as well as Women's Liberation, which has moved from being an Idea to being a *Movement*.

"The difference between the Women's Liberation Movement of the early twentieth century and that of the last two decades," she insists, "is that today's movement, by being rooted in *the movement from practice to theory which is itself a form of theory,* calls for a new relationship of theory to practice, from which a new Man/Woman relationship is certainly not excluded. On the contrary, it is integral *in* the revolution and the day *after* power is won."[13]

How terribly lonely these women must have been within the overwhelmingly male revolutionary movements. I referred earlier to Alexandra Kollontai. Like Raya Dunayevskaya, she thought, wrote, and acted out of a feminist vision. Her life, a generation before Raya's, was circumscribed by an even greater set of limitations. Nevertheless, she became the only woman member of the Bolshevik Central Committee and the USSR's first Commissar of Social Welfare. The ups and downs of her life are a poignant example of what today, so many years later, still tends to happen to brilliant, strong, visionary women within the revolutionary struggles they themselves initiate and help to win.

Kollontai, originally Alexandra Mikhailovna Domonotivich, was born in 1873. She studied political economy in Switzerland, taught in workers' schools, participated in international socialist conferences, and wrote on socialism and political economy. She worked on women's suffrage with Clara Zetkin, knew Rosa Luxemburg, Karl Kautsky, and Georgi Plekhanov. Her work with women was many-pronged. She eventually joined the Bolshevik Party. In March 1917 she was elected to the executive committee of the Supreme Soviet, and in August of that year to the Communist Party's Central Committee.

After the October Revolution, Kollontai was named Commissar of Social Welfare. Between 1918 and 1926, new laws on marriage, divorce, and guardianship were passed, and abortion was legalized. A birth control clinic was opened in Moscow. Remember, we are talking about the earliest decades of this century. Feminist issues were important in the initial revolutionary program, but then reaction set in. When Stalin rose to power, most of the feminist gains were repealed. Abortion became illegal in 1936, and remained so until 1955, one year before the famous Twentieth Congress.

Kollontai was soon appointed ambassador to Norway and Mexico, where she was effectively removed from the center of ideological struggle. Well aware that being sent so far away would silence discussion of her ideas, she began to put those ideas into a series of important writings, including two novels, *Love of Worker Bees* and *A Great Love*. Kollontai did not live to see the beginning of the thaw; she died of a heart attack in 1952.[14]

What were some of the so-called objective factors that provoked the retreat from egalitarian values in the

Soviet Union? One was the imposing economic project: how to bring a feudal society into the twentieth century, with all the problems of archaic methods of production and distribution, natural disasters, failed crops, and tens of thousands of starving people. Lacking a long-range view, it must have seemed expedient to sacrifice the more complicated superstructural changes and concentrate on all-out efforts in production.

The capitalist world also quickly isolated the first country to attempt a socialist revolution. And in the Soviet Union, the hardships of revolution were followed by the rigors of World War II, in which our Soviet allies lost 20 million citizens. Quickly, defense as well as production became a priority. A "first things first" attitude always has a ready-made place in the context of such an intense struggle for survival. Yet these explanations, real and oft-repeated as they are, don't present the whole picture. The history of women's oppression is more complex.

At least two decades of extreme authoritarianism followed Stalin's rise to power from the early 1920s, when he became general secretary of the Communist Party, to the early 1950s, when he stepped down as premier of the Soviet Union. Along with tens of thousands of lives, many aspects of the Bolshevik dream were stifled or destroyed during this time. When stock was taken at the Twentieth Congress in 1956 some specific errors were rectified. But while *particular* changes were made, such as legalizing abortion, why was the problem of *how* things got so skewed never adequately addressed? In an immense country with an exceedingly top-heavy bureaucracy, it isn't easy to unravel years of error. But much of the problem was certainly the familiar inability to attend to process.

I would suggest that another reason there wasn't a more useful analysis may have been the fact that a single man, Stalin, became the scapegoat for all that had gone wrong. This tendency, too, has male overtones, in which men respond more to a product-oriented mind-set than to the more female concern with process. Josef Stalin was certainly a dictator, an architect of an atmosphere of terror that should have no place in a socialist vision. But social ills can never be attributed to a single person. The failure to look deeper and address ideological and cultural issues only allows the problems to reappear.

Life for women in the Soviet Union has been contradictory under a top-heavy and collapsing socialism, and this is particularly evident since the country's turn toward a market economy. Compared to their situation in Czarist Russia, women obviously gained a great deal from revolutionary change. And yet women have been the ones who have most passionately defended *glasnost* and *perestroika*. Feminist Alexandra Muzirya tells us that "when tanks lumbered through the streets of Moscow, it was the women who turned confrontation into communication . . . began direct dialogue with the soldiers . . . openly called upon the young men to 'unite with the people.' "[15]

But Muzirya also concedes that "the rise of democracy in the Soviet Union. . . damaged the status of women." She says women lost almost half their seats on the Supreme Soviet and even more in the parliaments of the various republics. During the socialist era, female representation in politics was determined by a quota. It was mandatory that 30 percent of the top positions in the Presidium of the Communist Party and the Assembly of Ministers go to women. Of course these were women approved by the male power structure. This is where one understands, again, that being female does not automatically make one a feminist. Still, 30 percent signals a *potential* we have yet to approach in the United States.

The current attempt at transition to a market economy, Muzirya explains, has also brought a reduction in middle-echelon administrative positions, threatening jobs held by women. And the economic changes, with their attendant transitional crises, have made daycare and other services more expensive. Here again we are witnessing a situation in which the laws benefiting women—fought for and won, at least on paper, during the socialist era—will be put to a reality test through the struggles provoked in this period of extreme upheaval.

Slavenka Draculić, author of *How We Survived Communism and Even Laughed*—a book more thoughtful than its title implies—describes succinctly and dramatically what the turn towards market economies is beginning to mean for women in Eastern Europe.[16] Upon receiving a rather post-modernist questionnaire from a U.S.

feminist, she composed the following (unsent) response:

> Dear B, we live surrounded by newly opened porno shops...unemployment, and galloping poverty . . . Rumanian women are prostituting themselves for a single dollar in towns on the Rumanian-Yugoslav border . . . our anti-choice nationalist governments are threatening our right to abortion and telling us to multiply, to give birth to more Poles, Hungarians, Czechs, Croats, Slovaks. We are unprepared, confused, without organization or movement yet. . . . A Critical Theory approach? Maybe in ten years. In the meantime, why don't you try asking us something else?[17]

Losing their social gains and besieged by pornography, there is certainly abundant evidence that the turn from a socialist form of government has not been wonderful for women.

Listen to Muzirya again, this time quoting from a speech given by Marina N. Rakhmananova at the September 3, 1991, Congress of People's Deputies:

> We had a very sad impression . . . that future congresses are going to be made up only of men . . . we have only men playing a role . . . they have slogans, they make *coups d'état*, but there are things that are more important than politics, such as human rights and morality and economy... Women are the conscience of the nation. The woman is responsible for morality in the family, but we do not see this manifested in society. One of the reasons for this lack of morality in our society today is the lack of contribution by women.

Rakhmananova goes on to speak about men's decision to send their sons to Afghanistan, about men making all the plans, solving all the problems. She ends with a plea for a separate body of women lawmakers: "This may seem funny at first glance, comrades, but many of our poets are saying that this is a good idea. This is not to compete with you, but to ensure that the whole society is saved so that the sensible, sober voice of the woman should make itself felt in our political life."

This plea, reminiscent in form and content to Abigail Adams's letter to her husband in the early years of our own colonies, bears sad witness to how little we've really gained. Although drawing upon the wisdom of poets to support women's separate political space may appear romantic or irrelevant, it strikes a chord in me. Rakhmananova seems to be making a connection between poetry's nonlinear structure and the more creative, critical, and process-oriented direction that women can bring to problem-solving. She understands that in her national history, at least, the quota system has not respected women's contribution. On the contrary, it has coopted that contribution. As has been true in other times and places, women need to develop a strength outside the male power structure in order to bring to bear our full potential.

Now that the Soviet Union has decreed itself out of existence, replacing the state that was born of the 1917 Revolution with a commonwealth of independent nations, the maneuverings of an "ol' boy's" club headed by Yeltsin are much easier to see. Yeltsin became the man in charge largely because he proved to be the one most able to play by Western rules. No women's voices have sounded in the forefront of current Soviet politics, although many women in Russia and the other republics must be making their own assessment of what is happening and of how the various changes will help or hurt women's lives. As power is consolidated and choices are made, women will undoubtedly continue to struggle for their place.

History shows us how difficult this has always been. Forced to defend themselves against hostility from within as well as from outside, victorious revolutionary movements have generally reverted to the comfort of familiar ways: men providing the ideas and action, women "fearlessly" supporting them. The "safety" of the nuclear family has been seen as refuge. Women and other "minorities" were *granted* certain improvements in their conditions of life, but never themselves permitted to be the real agents of change.

Some continue to claim that the effort to effect a change in consciousness is too costly, or too divisive of the rank and file who supposedly, after all, know and care little about anything besides decent working conditions, a livable wage, and acquiring some measure of dignity in their lives, food on the table and such essentials as shelter, health, and education. Mediocre leadership lacks a respect for and confidence in ordinary people. Too often those with the power to define our lives conceive of dignity, health, and education timidly and without vision.

With the survival of the revolution at stake, once again complex discussions were put off and reeducation necessary for the development of a new and more humanitarian view of human relations postponed. *There will be time enough later . . .* has always been the refrain. But within one or two generations, this failure fully to address issues of consciousness has ended up coming back like a contaminated boomerang to taint socialist revolutions. It seems to me that the failure of these revolutions to develop an authentic feminist agenda, as well as their unwillingness to address other superstructural issues, has seriously affected their ability to survive.

The first socialist revolution, in the early years of this century, was still relatively young when the world was battered by a succession of wars. The most devastating was World War II, with its aftermath of political conservatism. As the superficial and repressive 1950s began to recede, movements intent upon revolutionizing human consciousness proliferated in the West. They sprang up in a variety of contexts and flourished, particularly in the Paris and Prague springs of 1968, in Mexico City that same year, and in the United States throughout the late 1960s and 1970s.

In the United States, these were years of extraordinary struggle for change on the part of blacks and other "minorities"—women, homosexuals, and the differently-abled. Movements of consciousness grew into battles for survival and empowerment. Groups concerned with the destruction of our habitat emerged and tried to promote a more holistic view of the earth and human wellness. The aged and also the very young began to speak out for their particular needs. The peace movement flourished.

The very concept of minority is disempowering to any people so categorized; and it's worth noting that while those in power continue to use the term, people of color are actually the vast majority of the world's population. In places like South Africa, blacks are so obviously the majority that the minority whites have had to look to other stigmatizing terms to justify their racist rule.

For North Americans, these years were most profoundly marked by the civil rights and black liberation movements, massive protests against the Vietnam war, the first successful socialist revolution in the American hemisphere (Cuba), the explosive beginnings of the second wave of feminism, a resurgence of the Native American and Chicano struggles, the battle for Puerto Rican independence, and the Stonewall riot that gave birth to gay liberation.

Legislation was rewritten to reflect this spreading consciousness, and in many instances new laws were passed. U.S. Supreme Court decisions such as Brown *v.* Board of Education and Roe *v.* Wade, to name only those that have become household references, marked the culmination of decades of people's struggle and defined an era whose gains seem frighteningly precarious today. Civil rights and affirmative action were dignified by law. Women fought for and won a measure of control over our bodies. The academy was forced to open itself to different ways of teaching literature and the social sciences. In response to urgent student demand, black studies, women's studies, Native

American and Chicano studies were offered on college campuses across the country. Public services became more responsive to the needs of the disadvantaged.

Although they never fail to crack down when necessary, the ruling classes in the industrially developed nations, faced with the example of socialism over ever greater areas of the globe, in general preferred to allow a certain margin of tolerance for these movements and their gains. This tolerance itself was pointed to as evidence of democracy (appearance is always more important than substance, for the dominant class). And as long as such struggles didn't threaten the power structure, they could be absorbed. To some degree they were seen as a buffer against real structural change.

In the United States today we are experiencing a frenzy of carefully nurtured addictions as well as a rise in fundamentalism and neofascism and a backlash of conservative power, robbing us of many of the rights we believed we had achieved in perpetuity. In Eastern Europe and other independent nations that were once part of the Soviet Union, Grenada, several of the African and Asian nations, Nicaragua, and elsewhere, long-time socialist or socialistic experiments have caved in to covert and overt pressures. The peoples of these countries tell us they want the freedoms we enjoy, and that their "choice" of a market economy and a democracy which looks like ours will provide them with those freedoms.

In the one-time socialist world we were told that people's disaffection was triggered by increased economic crises and their inability to acquire the lavish comforts and commodities so seductively advertised under capitalism, and by the lack of individual freedoms that others in the more industrialized societies struggled for and won. Irresponsible media coverage has made it difficult to follow a logical history. President Bush and our national newscasters spoon-feed a package of explanations to middle Americans conditioned to expect and applaud the failure of anything that challenges our definition of democracy.

But these explanations are not consistent with my experience. I lived in Cuba for ten years of its socialist process. For another four I shared the Nicaraguan Revolution, which although not cast in a traditional socialist mold nonetheless drew on socialist principles for its program.[18] I am filled with memories of life in Cuba and Nicaragua. Now these memories struggle for expression. I want to be able to articulate them fully at this time, when conformity urges people to accept the inevitable demise of socialism.

When I think of my life in Cuba, I recall the ease and relief of a mother raising four children in a country where a job was assured; where health care, education, recreation, and culture were all free; and where our youngsters could play and grow without fear of violence or drugs. I remember the enthusiasm and pride we shared when every Cuban adult completed the equivalent of a sixth grade education, or what it felt like to dig potatoes on a Sunday afternoon and then find them plentiful and cheap in the market Monday morning, a clear result of one's personal contribution to collective labor. Nothing will wipe from my memory the joy Nicaraguan women experienced when their government issued a decree forbidding images of the female body in commercial advertising, or the pride my daughters felt as they joined volunteer coffee brigades or taught adults reading and math.[19] What a crime that so many tangible accomplishments, benefiting peoples in countries with a history of poverty, have been erased to the tune of "democracy's triumph." As people cheer "the death of socialism" without a knowledge of what socialism can be, the loss of all this and so much else brings a very real ache to my breast and tears to my eyes. I will not swallow the flippant stories, but rather will question and look for answers of my own.

And I will continue to wonder why socialist revolutions consistently fail to develop an autonomous feminist discourse, a process of feminist agency. Don't get me wrong. I believe *all* of these revolutions helped to produce a better life for women. What I am talking about, in its most profound, all-encompassing definition, is a feminist discourse based on an ideology embracing democratic relations of power, a redefinition of history and of memory, and a world view that favors life over the signs of imminent death that we experience on so many fronts.

In a matter of months, we have seen socialist governments topple in Eastern Europe and in the Soviet Union. It has happened through bloody civil war (Romania and then Yugoslavia), almost peaceably

(Czechoslovakia, Bulgaria), or with an orchestrated "unification" that outdid any Cecil B. De Mille extravaganza (East Germany). Frequently these collapses followed the consequent breakup of republics and regions, often along ethnic lines. (Are unresolved racism and a disrespect for cultural autonomy the issues here?) For women these changes hardly lessened the institutionalized discrimination or sexist attitudes.

In June 1991, the first international meeting of the Network of East-West Women met in Dubrovnik, Yugoslavia, composed of forty-five women from Bulgaria, Romania, Czechoslovakia, Poland and the former German Democratic Republic and fifteen veteran U.S. feminists.[20] They shared a bleak panorama. Historian and feminist Ruth Rosen, who attended the meeting, heard Sonja Lict, a Yugoslavian feminist sociologist, warn that "the revolutions of 1989 are incomplete," describing them as "male democracies." A Czech journalist spoke of how all the ethnic groups in her country have tried to coerce women into raising the birth rate, painfully reminiscent of earlier historic episodes. "All these nationalistic groups view us as breeders, nothing more," she said.

A former head of Solidarity's women's bureau agreed. She explained that Solidarity has "capitulated to the Church and nationalistic yearnings to restore the traditional family"; she and others have been forced into retirement or obliged to quit their jobs. And a Yugoslavian writer explained that in her country "feminism is a four-letter word. Either it is contaminated by past associations with state-coerced labor or tarnished by media-generated distortions of Western feminism."

Rosen learned that the current "democratic" revolutions have at least one thing in common with the socialist revolutions. "When asked to support women's needs as housewives or workers, or to protect their reproductive choices," she found out, "the brave men who helped topple the old regimes now respond, 'We must build democracy first' . . . it used to be 'we must build socialism first'."

In the few remaining enclaves of a system that only a short time ago influenced half the world, countries like Cuba and North Korea are threatened as never before. The importance of the nonaligned movement has also diminished as the United States consolidates its hegemony. Grenada, Panama, and other recent examples of outright military invasion are memorable warnings to anyone who dares envision a society based on principles of independence and justice, or determined simply to become independent of superpower domination.

Analyzing the murder of socialism is not difficult: Each socialist experiment, by virtue of its own errors, violated many of the premises upon which it was constructed. While the United States was building long-range policies in search of a new world order, socialism's own accumulation of errors led to its suicide of sorts. Some have criticized this characterization as too strong. But I wonder. It is as a woman who still considers herself a socialist that I rage against stagnancy, criminal mismanagement, corruption, and neglect. Too many of those I loved became expendable by not selling out a vision that others sought to destroy. Too many millions in too many different countries are now being sacrificed in a desperate grab for Western markets, advertised as the cure for every ill. And the fact that capitalism itself is less and less able to address people's needs is seldom mentioned.

Among socialism's errors are the treatment of certain unexamined beliefs as if they were an immutable science, a self-induced blindness toward, and fear of, groups whose liberation struggles threaten traditional leadership (notably women and gays), duplicity in terms of the internal line on the one hand and what you tell the people you're organizing on the other, a democratic centralism that retains all of the centralism and little of the democracy, personality cults, new class privilege, cronyism, and much else.

In the struggle to oust dictatorships and escape colonial or imperialist control in the consolidation of these socialist systems, feminism never stood a chance. Why have women's struggles for memory and self-determination fared so badly in the many efforts to construct a more just society?

Before my move to Managua, I lived in Cuba from 1969 to 1980, where my life focussed to a great extent on feminist concerns. I raised four children while working at a variety of jobs. I engaged in the many different discussions about women's changing roles in Cuban society and whether the revolution did or did not support a feminist agenda. I wrote several books and numerous articles based upon my observations of and participation in the Cuban process, of which I will say more.[21]

Now I note my own use of the phrase *women's changing roles*. It's interesting. Why do we always speak of a woman's role as one that must change? Why do we not assume that men must change when the social configuration does not work? This pervasive sense of men as center and women as adjunct, or other, is at the root of what authentic feminist discourse is all about. And this imbalance damages collective as well as individual memory.

In the late summer of 1974, I was invited by the Vietnamese Women's Union to what was then the Socialist Republic of North Vietnam. I traveled through the countryside and to the liberated zone of Quang Tri, just south of the 17th parallel. This was a nation at war, immersed in a lengthy and exceptional struggle. My visit took place a short six months before the Vietnamese defeated the United States and reunified their country. Again, the purpose of my trip was to interview women, and a small book resulted from that journey.[22] So in Vietnam, too, I was able to think a great deal about what socialism can mean for women's lives.

I cannot say whether I understand in detail how socialism was structured in Vietnam or in every sense how it affected women. But I can speak of how moved I was by an elderly Vietnamese woman, a party cadre, whose life had been given to struggle. She is someone I never want to forget. This woman, who was in her late seventies, still traveled about the countryside talking to others who were exploited like herself, and to the men who oppressed them. She told me about brigades of older women who went around teaching younger women how to recognize and honor their feelings, how to stand up for their needs, and fight for their rights. Together they reasoned with the men. And if reason didn't work, they resorted to the creativity of stronger methods.

To my admittedly outsider's eye, the Vietnamese were particularly able to combine changes in human consciousness with a changed relationship to production, while tirelessly defending their nation. Sitting under a shady willow tree one day, in the bombed-out ruins of what had once been a city, another woman told me about her father's several wives, and the revolution's campaign against polygamy. In Vietnam, one of the things I learned, again, was that people are defined by their history and culture; and that socialism, as elsewhere, is no more a unified system than is capitalism.

# 4
## CUBA . . .

The revolution gave human beings their dignity back; it didn't just give it back to men. Because I don't believe that the words *man* or *men* include women. I don't agree that when one is going to talk about human beings one should say *men*. I don't think men would agree that our saying *women* when what we mean is men and women really includes them.

**—Haydée Santamaría, 1979**[1]

Although that 1974 visit afforded me a brief look at how socialism had changed women's lives in North Vietnam, my Cuban experience was much more complete. There I participated in the extraordinary ways a people go about trying to change society in so many of its vital areas: throwing off the domination of a power like the United States that keeps you down so that its own elite may enjoy a better life, while at the same time attempting to discard various home-grown oppressions. My decade of life and work in Cuba was my first opportunity to live the complexities and contradictions inherent in the task of changing women's lives. It was also my first taste of what the achievements

121

might look like. *Marxism in Spanish*, we laughingly called it back then.

Cuban revolutionaries consider the necessities of life as rights, not privileges reserved for a very few. Extraordinary successes during the years I lived in Cuba included eradicating unemployment and providing shelter, health care, education, recreation, and culture to everyone—as *integral parts of life* rather than as luxuries available only to those who can afford them. Food and other goods were distributed equitably. Back then, although you might not be working at the job of your choice, you were working. No one was left without adequate medical or dental attention. Many homes were overcrowded, but new housing was going up everywhere and no one was homeless. Nor were there great numbers of beggars as in the rest of Latin America or on the streets of New York City—a situation many in today's United States would find enviable.

Faced with a continued economic blockade and hostility from the United States, Cuba has become increasingly isolated since the collapse of the socialist world. Relying on tourism for much of its hard currency, the country has seen a revival of some of the problems previously eradicated by the revolution: a resurgence of prostitution (especially in the port areas and around the luxury hotels), an active black market, and an increase in crime. Many of the achievements which I speak about in the following pages are being threatened as the revolution struggles to survive. Still, the tally is impressive. Against formidable odds, Cuba has managed to retain its major socialist gains.[2] The average life expectancy is seventy-five years, as opposed to sixty-two before the revolution. The overall sixth-grade education enjoyed by adults when I lived there has since gone up to eighth grade (it was second grade before 1959). Through a program of profound economic transformation, Cuba now produces eight times the energy it produced before, fourteen times the oil (10 percent of its total consumption), ten times the steel, eight times the eggs. There are twenty-six times more schools, eleven times more universities, and nine times more doctors. Today 70 percent of the machinery used in a Cuban sugar mill (sugar is the country's basic crop) is produced inside the country. What other underdeveloped third world nation can say as much?

The U.S. economic blockade remains the single most difficult obstacle to economic growth and prosperity, indeed to the very survival of the revolution. Although Cuba now shows a 6 percent unemployment rate (it was virtually zero when I lived there), this largely represents farm workers or those who are unwilling to accept jobs outside their professions. The country has added to its social infrastructure by building highways and dams, improving the public transportation system, building new housing, and spending a considerable percentage of its yearly budget on health and education. Reliance on Soviet oil was, unfortunately, great and its loss has called for heroic measures— thousands of bicycles have replaced automobiles and teams of oxen are used where there is no gas for tractors. Surviving the current "special situation" will depend in large part upon how quickly the government is able to establish new trade partners and how willing the Cuban people are to continue making enormous sacrifices. Cuba's current annual deficit is $2 billion, and there is the problem of surplus currency (more money than goods).[3]

But the Cuban Revolution did not only attend to a transformation in the base, changes in consciousness have also been important. A people's history, ignored or mis-represented over and over, generation after generation, was retrieved and disseminated with pride. Yet even this new history is most often told from a male perspective, and although sometimes includes *more* women, it is rarely from a feminist standpoint. This, of course, is part of the problem. In any case, extraordinary feats were ac-complished in the face of constant harassment from the United States: economic blockade, military attack, ideological, diplomatic, and every other kind of warfare. To date, Cuba has almost miraculously withstood more than three decades of hostility from the North.

In my own life and in the lives of my children, I saw what the Cubans were able to do to rout institutional-ized racism. I saw the profound changes in the lives of women who benefited from innovations in education, and marveled at a publishing program that had people lining up for books that cost less than a loaf of bread. Their editions numbered in the tens of thousands for a population of only 11 million. My kids went to schools where manual and intellectual work were combined to give students a more holistic sense of themselves and the world around them. There were numerous daily examples of what it meant to live in a producer rather than a consumer society.

My daughter Ximena recovered her hearing and survived a life-threatening illness because of an operation that would have cost many thousands of dollars in the United States. In Cuba it was free. I had a kidney removed shortly after my arrival in 1969, also at no monetary cost to myself. If a family member needed an operation but couldn't provide the hospital with the customary payment of one donated pint of blood, well that was all right too. The local Defense Committee (CDR) was happy to sign off that for whatever reason the donation hadn't been possible.[4] No one went without help.

But this same daughter complained bitterly about our first Christmas on the island, when she discovered that the cowgirl suit she had chosen as her special present came without the toy gun and hat included in the version sold for boys. For this holiday, rationing permitted every child in the country one toy worth more than three pesos and two worth less. There was no argument capable of effecting a switch, and Ximena's frustration was compounded by the fact that Cuban women served in the armed forces and militia, and were encouraged to break with so many traditional limitations. Why should she have been satisfied with a gender-specific cowgirl suit? Several years later the revolution too reflected upon this absurd division of toys and the restrictions were lifted.

I share not only the facts—statistics that are impressive by any measuring rod—but these aspects of socialist society which I experienced because it's important to keep them in mind. Vague references to "the failure of communism" or "the change to a market economy," so in vogue today, obscure the ways in which a socialist structure translates into the everyday lives of ordinary people. In our press there is endless discussion about socialism's insoluble problems, as if capitalism had none. The goal and processes of socialism, conceived of and inhabited by human beings, are rarely if ever mentioned. By the time I arrived in Cuba, women slightly outnumbered men in the schools of engineering, architecture, medicine, and other fields previously closed to them. Women earned the same as their male counterparts in comparable jobs, enjoyed maternity leaves similar to those in the Scandinavian countries, and received yearly pap smears through the neighborhood defense committees that greatly reduced the incidence of death from cervical cancer. Although still few in numbers, women also held high-level political and administrative positions. Yet I remember a friend, a woman in her late forties, telling me that when she went out to do volunteer work she changed from a skirt into pants and back into a skirt again at her place of employment; she didn't want to subject her very elderly parents to the shock of seeing her "dressed like a man."

As a woman who had only a year or so before discovered feminism, and as a poet and oral historian for whom people's stories, opinions, and ideas were deeply important, the Cuban Revolution's ways of dealing with feminist issues and its concepts of criticism/self-criticism were particularly interesting to me. I had come, after all, from the United States, and more recently from Mexico, two countries where feminism was hardly high on the list of official concerns.[5]

From my first days in Cuba, it was easy to see how the revolution had changed things for women. I'll never forget the response of a woman who cleaned the floors in the hospital were I had my kidney removed. When I asked what socialism had meant to her, she said "Honey, I married for love! The revolution made it possible for me to divorce a husband I wasn't happy with, work to support myself, and marry for love!" Everywhere, women glowed with the joys of their newly won social place.

In Cuba in the 1970s, almost no one I knew talked about being gay. It was too dangerous. Since then, conditions and attitudes about homosexuality have improved. Still, as recently as 1992, a close friend who is a lesbian avoided using the word in a letter to me. She described herself as "someone who belongs to one of those groups not favorably looked upon," spoke of her thirteen-year relationship with "una amiga"—a woman friend—and went on to say that although professionally she had become quite successful, it was "a difficult struggle all the way."

But things are changing. A letter to Boston's *Gay Community News* from two San Francisco-based lesbians provides some encouraging insights into Cuba's official attitude toward gay lifestyles. It's a long letter, but two of its paragraphs are worth quoting in full:

> In the early 1970s, the National Commission of Sex Education (CNES), a government-funded program, was formed to research and do wide-spread outreach on various sex education issues. In recent years, the CNES has made a commitment to countering homophobia and educating people to realize that homosexuality is a healthy option. So far, they have specifically focused on outreach to doctors, mental health professionals, and schools. They also encourage the family of gay people to go to family therapy in order to understand, accept and support their gay children . . . several years ago, the government passed a directive making it illegal to harass anyone on the street for their appearance, clothing or behavior. This was especially important for gays and lesbians, as there were incidents of police harassment in the past.

This letter also tells us that

> Currently there is a discussion group going on at the University of Havana about gay and lesbian issues. As well, the premiere of a play about the friendship between a gay man and a young Communist activist, *La catedral del helado* [The Ice Cream Cathedral], by Senal Paz, has been selling out for the past month. People, gay and straight, stand in line for several hours to get tickets. We had the opportunity to see the play. It was thrilling to witness the passionate standing ovation the audience gave the performer. The play has received great reviews applauding its confrontation of prejudice against gay people . . .[6]

Although the Cubans have a long way to go before

ridicule of and hostility toward gays are routed from their culture, it doesn't surprise me that this type of frontal attack on homophobia and heterosexism is taking place within a revolutionary society. Hopefully it won't be too long before the gay man and the young communist activist on the Cuban stage may be one and the same person.

When I arrived in Havana in 1969, I went to work in publishing. I soon presented to my immediate boss, a member of the military, my proposal for a book about women. Although that too was a difficult economic period, this man approved the project and encouraged me. For the next two years, I was paid to listen to women's stories, analyze their experiences, and think about how Cuba's brand of socialism affected their lives.

There were women among the star cane-cutters, a job as excruciating, back-breaking, and dirty as any I've known. Some cut as much and as fast as the men, then proudly showed off long painted fingernails and freshly curled hair when they came in from the fields. Other women, in an attitude of resistance to the U.S. economic blockade, made eye shadow out of pastel chalks, or drew black lines with an eyebrow pencil down the backs of their calves to simulate the nylon stockings they could not buy. Female ingenuity didn't always take the form that a feminist from the United States might have expected.

Through education, the labor force, and protective legislation, and in services such as daycare, collective dining facilities and laundries—wherever women's general sense of self-worth was concerned—things in Cuba had changed enormously. The prevailing assumption was that institutionalized discrimination had virtually been eliminated. In fact, the term *institutionalized* was often used to differentiate between the revolution's program as set forth in laws, decrees, and educational campaigns—and the *residual* prejudice that no one denied still lurked in people's minds.

From time to time during my years in Cuba I witnessed interesting struggles in the context of Cuban cultural history. In the mid-1970s, a ten-minute film called *El piropo* ("The Catcall") glorified—indeed, immortalized—the numerous "creative" ways in which men verbally assault (approach, demand attention from, comment upon, hoot at, or joke about) women in the streets. In the film, the practice was viewed as a cultural phenomenon worthy of appreciation. It catered to a particular Cuban and very male sense of humor, with nothing resembling a feminist point of view. There was almost no public outcry.[7]

El *piropo* particularly provoked me, and I began making it my business to stop and challenge the men who called me *chula* or remarked upon the size of my thighs or asked if I wanted to come home and "do it" with them. I remember that my two oldest daughters, vulnerable teenagers at the time, became especially wary of going for walks with me; and when they did, stayed at a distance if I decided to engage a man in this way.

But more often these were fruitful encounters. I would ask one of these guys how he thought his mother or sister or girlfriend would feel if addressed by men as if she were a piece of meat. Most of them stopped, actually gave the question some thought, and frequently agreed that it was not revolutionary behavior. (As I write, I am struck by the similarity between my approach and that of my son when he worked to dissuade his classmate from delinquency!) I won't claim that my challenge will change the way these men conduct themselves, but it did make many of them stop and think.

This could never have happened in any other Latin American country, including Mexico where I had lived for eight years. I knew the dangers I would have incurred if I had tried it there. The Cuban Revolution, with its serious formulation of women's rights, provided the context for considering every *human* need. Insofar as women are also human, it wasn't that difficult to discuss the inappropriate behavior of approaching us as if we could be taken and used. Such extraordinary progress was being made in many areas. Why couldn't the revolution have risked going further?

Several years later, another film challenged the prevailing male attitudes about women. It was a full-length feature called *Portrait of Teresa*. I remember heterosexual couples leaving the theater after seeing the film. Sometimes the woman and man stalked off angrily in opposite directions. *Portrait of Teresa* deals with a husband's jealousy of his wife's political and cultural activities, both in terms of her necessarily diminished caretaking within the family, and in the context of the competitive disadvantage he feels because of her greater social participation. She rebels. The film has an intentionally ambiguous ending, which provoked much public discussion.

The Federation of Cuban Women (FMC), a mass organization founded in August 1961 and eventually enlisting more than 80 percent of the country's female population above the age of 14, was and is controlled by the Cuban Communist Party. The feminist discourse that might have addressed these issues *from the unique experience of women ourselves* was never really encouraged. Although the FMC coordinates an extraordinary female force, like AMNLAE in Nicaragua (and for similar reasons) it has been much more successful at organizing women in support of the revolution than in raising a feminist agenda. While the issue of an autonomous women's organization was frequently debated (but not adopted) in Sandinista Nicaragua, in Cuba it was never mentioned, at least not publicly.

"You can't change these things overnight," was something you often heard, sometimes by way of honest explanation, often with evident relief. *Residual sexism* was how the Cubans referred to whatever discrimination against women was still apparent. The word *residual* seemed to indicate something very small, the mere shadow or taint of old ways. It was something left over. It would disappear. The classic Marxist concept was that equality would come as a result of more

egalitarian economic relations. And that once women—
or blacks, or any other group for that matter—had
gained economic equality, the rest would follow.

With slight variations, "progress will come as a result
of changes in the relations of production" became the
party line on women's equality in most if not all of the
socialist or revolutionary societies. The Vietnamese and,
of course, the Chinese parties placed more emphasis on
ideological struggle and the need to alter attitudes
rooted in centuries of patriarchy. In both these
countries, however, I would argue that *women's lives were
changed to better serve the goals of the revolution, not for their
own self-realization*. None of these revolutions encouraged the development of a feminist discourse that
allowed for any real female autonomy.

There is no question in my mind that in all these
experiments life improved for everyone, including
women. We mustn't make the mistake of comparing the
quality of life in the socialist and capitalist societies,
with no allowance for how the capitalist class structure
allows a few to live in luxury at the expense of the many
who live poorly and then evens it all out in some misleading statistic called "overall standard of living."

More appropriate comparisons would be Russia
under the czars with the Soviet Union after the Bolshevik Revolution, China in feudal times with China
after 1949, Cuba's pre-1959 misery with Cuba under
Fidel Castro, Nicaragua throughout the long Somoza
dynasty with that country during the Sandinista administration. But no matter how many arguments are

offered to the contrary, the continuing second-rate citizenship of women in all these countries is evidence to me that a profound women's revolution has yet to be made. And I would argue, especially in light of recent events, that stifling women's expression helped to bring most of these revolutions down.

It was the same refrain throughout the socialist world: once economic equality was achieved, the rest would follow. This *rest* was rarely if ever named. If you demanded space for a discussion of feminism, or encouraged an analysis based on the retrieval of women's history, women's culture, and women's experience, you would most likely be dubbed a "bourgeois feminist"—divisive, or worse, counterrevolutionary.

In Latin America during the 1970s, some of the New Left organizations did make progress toward questioning this line. The Tupamaros in Uruguay, the Chilean Movement of the Revolutionary Left (MIR), and other groups began to address the issue, but discussion generally didn't go much further than some excellent essays written by some extraordinary women.[8] There were a few dramatic events, like one March 8 in the early 1970s, when the Tupamaros celebrated International Women's Day by springing a group of their female political prisoners and then leading blindfolded journalists to a press conference where they proclaimed (referring to the women), "We can't make the revolution without them!" Still, there was always the "we" and the "them."

In the United States during the same decade, left

radical women with a feminist consciousness grew tired of trying to struggle inside mixed organizations. When such struggles appeared hopeless, the women often split off to form or join their own movements for change. These experiences taught us that women-only space is absolutely necessary to be able to draw upon our history and strength, unhindered by men who would continue to make us *other*. In the task of changing the world, though, we must also develop strategies that include all those who live here.

"Once economic equality is secured, the rest will follow." Without honest inquiry, without courageous analysis, how could we know what this unnamed *rest* might look like? What might it mean, for example, in Cuban women's lives? During my decade in Cuba, the absence of support for a radical feminist discourse, *within the particular Cuban socioeconomic and cultural context*, should have been a warning to me. It was not. I remember traveling to Chile in October 1972, and arguing with my friend Emma Herrera.

Emma was a Uruguayan journalist who had been exiled in Cuba, where we'd met, and later went on to Chile. She said she understood radical feminism, understood the need to theorize women into the center. I disagreed. The agenda was beyond the limits set by the Marxist theory or practice of the times. We fought for most of the morning, then went out to look for sunglasses on the streets of a Santiago which, almost a year later to the day, would run with people's blood.

Emma was one of the few Latin American

theoreticians at that time who had a radical feminist analysis. I never saw her again. Several months after my visit she and her husband and infant daughter were in an automobile accident from which she never regained consciousness. At least she was spared the terrible knowledge of Chile's loss. The coup, her body's journey back to a conservative family in Montevideo, and the years intervened so that I would not hear about her after that. Later, though, in Nicaragua, I used the name Emma Herrera when writing about feminist issues. I missed Emma. I missed our discussions. And I was still asking questions in a discourse that was becoming more and more imperative.

If we ask how socialism failed feminism, we must also ask how feminism failed socialism, at least the most radical feminist thought that was pushed to new limits in countries like ours. Of course those feminists were not in power. But then, women in the socialist societies were not truly in power either, which was precisely the problem. Many of the most powerful feminist spokeswomen in the United States at that time warned against collusion with any movement dominated by men. These women were formulating theories about gender that informed the ways we saw ourselves. But they failed to understand that in any process of profound change, class and race (as well as other variables) must also be taken into account. Radical feminism's distrust of socialist revolutions, as well as socialism's failure to consider feminism in its radical dimension, created a vacuum in which neither side could learn from the other's insights—a vacuum exploited by a common enemy whose use of such phrases as "post-feminist" or "death of socialism" is designed to disempower all our dreams.

During the years I lived in Cuba, criticism was seen rather statically. One was free to criticize, but only within what was considered a "revolutionary" framework. "Inside the revolution, everything; outside the revolution, nothing," was a statement of Fidel Castro's that I defended at the time.[9] I still agree that criticism must come from a desire to make the revolution work, not from an effort to destroy it. Those who support a people's right to self-determination can and should be critical. Those whose accusations serve only to "prove" that a system is flawed obey interests that have nothing to do with honest criticism. On the other hand, *any* stifling of discourse will one day have its negative impact. When a nation is particularly vulnerable to attack, addressing this issue in practice has always been difficult. In such situations there may be no question that some curtailment is necessary—in the short run. In the long run, censorship inevitably backfires.

Periodically, during the ten years I was there, the degree to which straying from the party line was seen as provocative and counterrevolutionary became alarming to the more thoughtful members of the revolutionary leadership. Sometimes ideas that had previously been stifled were reluctantly but necessarily conceded to have been correct. In 1969-1970, one such idea was that it was possible to harvest 10 million tons of sugar-cane. Those brave enough to publicly express their doubts were considered defeatists and relegated out of sight. When the goal indeed proved impossible, and the economy had been badly damaged in the effort, those critics were invited back into the fold. Apology was public. But damage to the critical process had been done. The Cuban Revolution is extraordinary in its ability to admit mistakes and rectify them; it is slower to permit a critical discourse that encourages real debate and may help prevent such errors from being made.

I now see that a missing piece was men's ability to see beyond male privilege. Those in power, in all places and at all times, will go through veritable contortions to avoid sharing that power. In Cuba, what was lacking was an understanding of *process*, an ongoing and open-ended inquiry into the very nature of critical thought, the ideology of domination, and people's need for crea-tive growth and expression. Each generation's most courageous and audacious thinkers build upon the ideas of those who precede them. When the continuum is broken, loss to the process as a whole cannot be counted in years.[10] For women this is essential, because process is something we do especially well, yet we have quite literally been written out of the history of our own experience.

Cuban intellectuals have long been uncomfortable with the quality of their press, its officious editorials and simplistic presentation of the news. From time to time the more serious—and courageous—among them would be able to provoke a real look at the current state of criticism. When I lived in Cuba people were actively encouraged to put forth opinions, great debates would take place, with opposing views freely exchanged. But attention only to the *current* state of something precludes the *process* to which I refer. The discussions also took place within a carefully delimited framework. Certain topics remained off limits and, most importantly, there was no recognition of the need to develop a practice that people could trust.

In Cuba, this spiraling back and forth between open criticism and a tighter lid on ideas and opinions was generally a response to a perceived need to defend the revolution against outside attack. Periods of greater hostility brought greater defensiveness, demanding increased attention to the central task of defending the revolution. But what kind of a revolution, with what built-in flaws, were we defending?

I want to emphasize something that the revolution didn't seem to grasp—and which none of the socialist experiments, to my knowledge, understood: criticism isn't something people develop simply because officialdom says, "Okay, it's all right to be critical now. Go ahead, it's okay now." Real critical thought develops over many years. Each successive generation must grow up in an atmosphere that encourages questions and challenges all "truths" absolutely—the elasticity of mind and body that makes it possible to accept being wrong and so dare to be right, breaking qualitative as well as quantitative bounds.

Life got much better for the vast majority of people in Cuba and in other countries where a socialist revolution was in place. Life got better, but the word that was transmitted to such political advantage in the Western news media was that it was getting worse. In countries such as the United States we were treated to pictures of bleak cities with monotonous lines of people buying commodities of poor quality, envious of the consumer society on the other side of the iron or banana curtain or the Berlin Wall. These same images were also expertly packaged and sent back to the countries they claimed to describe, provoking social unrest and promises of greener pastures on "the other side."[11]

To change society is difficult, especially if it is done under constant threat of military hostility from the North, as well as by the United States's and other nation's pressure on international financial organizations. Many Cubans believe the stories of absolute freedom "over there." There have been periodic exoduses, including the famous 1980 Mariel boat lift in which 125,000 people left the island.

Western propaganda rarely mentions the fact that in Cuba people have homes. They have jobs. They eat, although admittedly without the variety available to a middle-class person in the United States. Their children go to school, and education is free, from grade school through university. People also have health care, security as they grow older, recreation, sports, poetry, art, and the excitement of creative discovery. This latter is one of the great magics of the Cuban Revolution.

My anger rises when the staid academic detractors on the outside point to one or another error, and with smug contempt even claim that the suicides of Haydée Santamaría or Oswaldo Dorticós are evidence of a process gone bad.[12] With the recent turn to "freedom," "democracy," and incipient market economies in the erstwhile socialist world, some of those who cried loudest for change are already beginning to bemoan their losses: employment, job security, health care, social services—and, yes, eventually poetry too. (I am reminded of Marina Rakhmananova's plea to the Russian Congress of People's Deputies for a separate body of women lawmakers, and her comment that "many of our poets are saying this is a good idea.") The ways in which the reunification of Germany (absorption of one Germany by the other?) has made second-class citizens of the East Germans is enough to illustrate the complexities inherent in this change.

Change, yes; but will a market economy save these societies from misery and alienation? Is our system, with its gender inequities, its classism, racism, sexism, heterosexism and other institutionalized injustices—its inability to provide homes and jobs, its diminishing social services, lack of a national health care plan, near collapse of the banks and serious recession—really the answer to people's needs?

Many of the *Marielitos* were shocked when they discovered that medical attention was neither automatic nor free in the United States.[13] Even these disaffected exiles, who are quick to tell you how much they hated the Cuban Revolution and are waiting only for Castro to fall from power or die, were born into a world with certain revolutionary expectations. They believed that at the very least they have a right to an education, to be healthy, and to work.

But what about the failures of these socialist experiments? We who believe in socialism, who work hard for it, and who will forever have imprinted upon our eyes the faces of our friends who died for it, how must we analyze these failures? Of course a succession of U.S. administrations actively undermined and attacked these systems for years. But what failures can be ascribed to the ways in which socialism developed and functioned? Dazzled by the obvious accomplishments, I for one did not stop to wonder if or where downfall might have been built into the system.

It is clear that socialism as we have known it has had great difficulty addressing issues such as steady economic growth, increased productivity, keeping people working at optimum efficiency in a noncompetitive market, and an equitable and efficient distribution of goods. Moral and material incentives, as well as various combinations of both, have enjoyed alternating support. Multiple nationalities and their inherent cultural differences have posed a continual problem to socialism, particularly where large numbers of a country's population belong to ethnic groups other than the majority.

Less acknowledged, but no less problematic, have been racism, sexism, homophobia, the way knowledge is defined and transmitted, and the lack of critical inquiry. People's spirituality has frequently been trampled or ignored. Psychology and other important disciplines have been rejected as "bourgeois," rather than revisioned with class, race, and gender consciousness, and harnessed in the service of working people.

One of Cuba's extraordinary contributions to world revolution has been internationalism—a commitment to giving technological, intellectual, and military aid to countries that request it. This is no Alliance for Progress, with $4 dollars taken out for every dollar put in. Thousands of Cubans fought, and hundreds died, in Angola and Ethiopia. I remember the massive practical and emotional support in Revolutionary Square when Fidel Castro spoke of Cuba's multiracial heritage: "We are not only a Latin American nation; we are also a Latin African nation," he said. "African blood runs abundant in our veins. . . . We are brothers and sisters of the Africans and for the Africans we are prepared to fight!"[14]

Internationalism has put Cuban construction workers in Grenada, teachers and doctors in Nicaragua, and all manner of technicians and consultants throughout the developing nations. They go respecting local customs, with their own food and equipment, never taking a salary from the host country—truly giving disinterested aid. I remember, in Cuba, when my youngest daughter Ana's fifth grade teacher volunteered to go as an internationalist to Nicaragua. It meant that another fifth grade teacher had to take on two whole classes that year, sixty students. Nevertheless, students, parents, and the overworked teacher herself all assumed the challenge with pride. We knew how much Nicaragua needed those teachers.

But perhaps internationalism has also been a kind of culprit in its inability to openly confront feminist issues. It sometimes has had as its corollary the effect of minimizing difference, ignoring the needs of particular groups in an effort to point out the similarities between peoples, our human condition and the generosity that moves us to provide for one another. Could it be that the needs of women, lesbians and gay men, or ethnic minorities with cultural specificities, have been sacrificed to the great emotional energy necessary to rally people from one underdeveloped nation to offer their expertise (or their lives) in another? Does an emphasis on internationalism as an essential revolutionary practice limit socialism's ability to focus adequately on the needs of different social groups? If so, we must begin to develop an internationalism that also values difference.

Again, these are issues which in traditional Marxist terms are seen as superstructural. Understanding the relationship between the superstructure and the base (relations of production) is necessary if we want to change society. And Marxists will insist that this relationship is dialectical. But the weight given to economic change has often rendered these other considerations invisible. Especially in times of danger when the revolution is threatened from outside or within, or in times of hardship when everyone must pull together, issues such as racism, feminism, sexuality, and criticism are seen as divisive and petit bourgeois, hopelessly out of step, irresponsible, and even counterrevolutionary.

After fifteen years of insisting that discrimination against women in Cuba had been successfully dealt with, something happened that brought the situation into sharper focus. In the mid-1970s the Cubans began experimenting with what for them was a new kind of democracy, a process through which delegates to local, regional, and provincial assemblies would be elected by popular vote. No outrageous campaign funds were permitted; a simple 8"x 10" photo and a few typewritten pages detailing background and experience introduced each candidate, who was then available to talk about the issues for a few hours one or two afternoons a week. A pilot project would be carried out in a single province, Matanzas, and the lessons of that experience drawn upon when the project was extended nationwide the following year.

By the time July 26, 1974—the Cuban revolutionary holiday—came around, the single-province process was complete. Fidel Castro, who always speaks to the people on that day, chose Matanzas as the place where he would discuss the experience. People were enthusiastic; everything seemed to have gone well. Except for one thing: of those nominated, only 7 percent had been women. And of the total delegates elected, a mere 3 percent were women. Something was clearly wrong. Faced with such evidence, no one could deny that discrimination against women still existed.

I remember the electricity in the air that day. In Cuba July 26th celebrations always include a distinguished invited guest. That year she was Nguyen Thi Dinh, vice commander in chief of the South Vietnamese army, which just two months earlier had liberated its people from a monstrous war. Thi Dinh was middle aged, small in physical stature, but immense in presence. She embodied women's strength, dignity, and courage. Castro reached down to this woman who was a foot and a half shorter than he and drew her closer to the podium. As he reiterated that women must lead the struggle for our own equality, she remained beside him: an example and a challenge that touched us deeply.

But in the Cuba of the 1970s, Castro's exhortation that women lead the struggle for our own equality faced the contradiction implicit in the Cuban revolutionary model. Its failure to develop a genuine and popular critical process greatly reduced the possibility that women—or anyone else—might question official assumptions. And its failure to develop an autonomous women's movement meant that no organizational form existed through which a different practice might have been encouraged. Until that day in the plaza, when Fidel Castro used the word *discrimination* in connection with women, popular recognition that such a thing existed had not even been articulated.

The Cuban revolutionary leadership was interested in understanding why female representation in the new People's Power had been so low. A multidisciplinary group of experts was dispatched to Matanzas. Large numbers of women and men were interviewed and the answer seemed unanimous: the infamous *second shift*. If women were expected to take full responsibility for housework and child care as well as hold jobs outside the home and lead active political lives, many were not eager to run for office as well.

This research produced a series of study materials that were read and discussed by men and women alike—in factories, offices, and neighborhoods, party cells, military units, and schools. Eventually a new family code was drafted, with tremendous input from people at all levels of society. The code established revolutionary standards for relations between men and women in heterosexual partnership—the obligations and rights of men, women, and children.

Clauses 25 through 28 of the code detailed men's responsibility for half the work of home and child rearing, and encouraged them to do everything possible so that their wives could study, enter the professions of their choice, and participate fully in politics, cultural activities, sports, recreation, or whatever else interested them. There's no doubt that this was a leap forward in gender relations within the Cuban revolutionary process. Still, the *mechanism* by which people might question their reality continued to be lacking.

More animated and perhaps more important than the formal discussions was the informal talk—on buses, in supermarkets, wherever people came in contact with one another. Women felt a sense of security knowing that the state supported their rights. There was educational value in opening such an important subject to broad discussion, focusing on an issue that had previously been ignored. But here, as in other areas, this was not really a struggle led by the affected group. Had it been, might it have been different? More, or less, far-reaching? Not limited to the rights of heterosexual women?

Generational considerations become important here. During the discussions of the family code, my four children were in school—two of them in junior high and high school. A revolutionary education, lacking in feminist concepts as it surely was, had nonetheless done a great deal to move young people to more egalitarian positions. I'm reminded of an incident that involved my daughter Sarah. She was at the Lenin, a boarding school for particularly bright students. A boy in one of the dorms apparently asked his girlfriend to iron his shirt. She refused, but the matter didn't end there. The girls got together, among them my daughter, in a campaign to get the male students to understand that this was unacceptable behavior. The kids approached equality from a humanistic point of view. Ripe terrain, I would have thought, for a feminist look at social issues.

In Cuba, I had my own experience as a woman in a heterosexual relationship, trying to address issues of equality in a society that emphasized production. At the time I had not yet discovered my lesbian identity. I lived with the father of my youngest daughter and he and I both worked full time. We had struggled to a point where he was as willing as I was to stay home from work with a sick child. Whoever judged her or his tasks that day to be the least pressing, we reasoned, would be the one to remain with the baby. But there were social considerations that made it difficult if not impossible for us to follow this personal choice.

*Emulación* (the socialist alternative to competition) was important in all Cuban workplaces, classrooms, military units and the like. Together, people decided upon goals and collectively helped each other achieve them. If my partner stayed with our daughter, his absence affected the goals set by his office mates and him, thus threatening their place in the whole emulative process. If I stayed home, the same was true. The difference was that in my case my co-workers understood. After all, I was a mother, wasn't I? It was only *natural* that my baby be sick once in a while. In my husband's case, understanding was much harder to come by. So inside the relationship, we had gotten to a point where we'd worked things out to our satisfaction. But faced with problems like these, the social pressures suffered by each of us were very different.

If the revolutionary party in power had been willing to support a feminist agenda, individual women and men would have felt more fully supported in our personal battles to challenge traditional ways of confronting these issues and relating to one another. Since it was unable, or unwilling, change was made—but never *structural* change.

In the attempt to construct a healthier society,

heterosexism is an impediment of grave dimensions. The denial of social space to homosexuals goes beyond the simple fact of one more group being denied its rights and cultural memory. Gay life profoundly threatens patriarchy, in which so much depends upon reproducing the nuclear family structure. Tolerance of and respect for diversity helps to shatter the imposition of a unit that has traditionally been oppressive to *all* women. The Cuban Revolution owes a debt to its gay women and men, and Cuban homosexuals have a great deal to offer the revolution.

When Cuban women are able to create an autonomous movement, they will go further in setting the terms of their full emancipation. I have no doubt that they will continue to defend revolutionary goals, at least those that translate into social justice, equality, and a healthy respect for difference. A much more complete sex education will undoubtedly be undertaken in the schools. Sexist images and jokes may be curtailed or eliminated. Perhaps more attention will be given to ecological concerns. I want to believe that when Cuban women wage their own struggle, the rights of lesbians in and out of partnership and of single heterosexual women will also be on the agenda. And that in the party as well as in government, many more women will occupy positions of power.

In October 1991 the Cuban Communist Party held its Fourth Congress in Santiago de Cuba, the eastern city at the foot of the Sierra Maestra mountains, the heart of struggle in the revolutionary war of 1956-1958. Now, in the midst of what is surely the worst economic and political crisis in the thirty-three years since the revolution came to power, the people of that old city once again took to the streets in support of "the miracle" Fidel Castro says is needed to assure the continuance of socialism.

The breakdown of the socialist camp has meant extreme hardship for the country, which, coupled with continued hostility and blockade from the United States, makes the small island nation ever more dependent upon its own limited resources.[15] Cubans are being asked, yet again, to tighten their belts and bear up under the multiple pressures and tensions of a society suffering agonizing austerity.

In this context, there are logical questions—inside and outside of Cuba—about an eventual transference of power, once Castro is too old to govern, or whether in fact he has been in power far too long. Exile forces, for the most part centered in Miami, range from those who still harbor absurd hopes about cruising in and taking over, to those who consider more intelligent and power-sharing options. But within the revolution there are signs that the effort to make necessary changes while still remaining a bastion of socialism in the hostile world has not yet been exhausted. Gillien Gunn, of the Carnegie Endowment for International Peace, argues that the CIA and others have exaggerated Cuba's dependence on the socialist bloc.[16]

Regarding some of the issues I have been discussing, the Fourth Congress reversed the party's three-decade-long prohibition of membership for those with religious beliefs. The party leadership is also younger now—56 percent of the Central Committee was newly elected, its 225 members averaging 47 years of age—and the working-class composition is higher.[17] Still, the thirty-eight women on the new Central Committee represent only 17 percent of the total, and the three women (out of a total of twenty-five) on the Politburo is 12 percent. Although infinitely better than the 2 percent female representation in the U.S. Senate, these figures are much too low.

Numbers don't tell the whole story though. They never do. Concepción Campa is a woman on the new Politburo whose life could not have been the same in prerevolutionary Cuba. She is the scientist who recently developed the vaccine against meningitis that the Cubans are exporting to a number of much more highly industrialized nations; she heads the prestigious Finlay Institute. Elected to the Central Committee were women like Rosa Elena Simeón, president of the Academy of Science, Yolanda Ferrer and Mónica Krauss, important feminist theoreticians, and Melba Hernández, one of the two women veterans of Moncada, the action that initiated the revolutionary movement in 1952 (Haydée Santamaría was the other). These women's lives speak eloquently of the difference the Cuban Revolution has made for women.

The 1990s have begun with a dramatic consolidation of power on the side of international monopoly capitalism. George Bush's new world order promotes pseudo-democracy, conservatism, fundamentalism, increased dependency for the smaller and poorer countries, and new and dangerous nationalistic movements that are already dotting the globe with painful civil wars. Fascism is on the rise, with an increase in authoritarianism as its microcomponent. For those few remaining experiments in justice, such as the Cuban Revolution, feminism must play an extraordinarily important role. In fact, its ability to develop a truly autonomous feminist agenda may be one of the deciding factors in whether or not the experiment will continue to live and grow.

# 5
# BRINGING IT ALL TOGETHER . . .

What remains in the vicious circle of repression [is] the true story, which has been suppressed in the body [and] produces symptoms so that it [can] at last be recognized and taken seriously. But our consciousness refuses to comply, just as it did in childhood—because it was then that it learned the life-saving function of repression, and because no one has subsequently explained that as grownups we are not condemned to die of our knowledge, that, on the contrary, such knowledge [will] help us in our quest for health.

**—Alice Miller**[1]

What is this knowledge that will help us in our quest for health? It cannot continue to be the compendium accumulated through centuries of androcentric, Eurocentric focus, for clearly that vision impedes our coming to terms with who we are. For men as well as women, it is not simply a matter of factoring in the female's eyes and hands. We cannot continue to build upon assumptions that are themselves skewed, off-center, broken.

In fact, this knowledge is often one that patriarchy has intentionally concealed, from those who have been victims of its abuses as well as from society as a whole. Woman abuse—whether it takes the form of incest, emotional badgering, or the ongoing repression of creativity—has been perpetrated and protected by men.

Women must fight our way through layers of erasure, lies, and cover-up, unfolding memory in the body as well as in the mind. Feminist therapy, including what I refer to as body work, helps immeasurably in the struggle.[2]

In *The Politics of Women's Biology* the feminist biologist Ruth Hubbard opens with a line that brings many readers up short, while producing the relief of instant identification in others.[3] Hubbard says: "Nature is part of history and culture, not the other way around." No statement makes more profoundly clear the far-reaching implications of a "knowledge" that has built and built again upon its own "original sin." Rediscovering our identity and centering the self require a re-evaluation that frequently stumbles over its own feet. Once on the journey, though, we must pick ourselves up, explore the reason for our fall, and keep on going—perhaps altering our direction. And in all sorts of arenas we are doing just that.

Because of socialism's commitment to economic equality and social services, women in the socialist countries, along with acquiring a class consciousness, expect the state to take responsibility for people's basic needs. Under capitalism—those who proclaim feminism dead notwithstanding—feminists have gone a long way toward building the autonomous movement necessary to authentic struggle.

In the capitalist countries we also have developed a greater collective awareness of the damage we sustain from a perpetuation of sexist attitudes. Certainly recent developments in feminist therapy have contributed a great deal to this consciousness. It, and the organizational skills we've honed along the way, linked to our socialist sisters' understanding of class and their knowledge of the need for the state to provide basic services, may be an excellent jumping off place for the coming global stage of struggle.

I look at the disasters in the Soviet Union, Eastern Europe, China, some of the African countries, Nicaragua, and Cuba, whose revolutionary survival now seems more threatened than ever. In the world's first Union of Socialist Republics it's only been a matter of weeks from statues of Lenin being ripped off pedestals to the fragmentation of the union itself. Events happen in such rapid succession that I am tempted to put this aside and wait for a period of stability in which to write: the proverbial distance from which to access what has been made and unmade. Distance itself can be dangerous, though, for memory and passion necessarily recede. I don't believe we can wait to address these issues—and I know we already have important things to say—so I continue to plunge ahead and take my chances.

There is the chaos, and there are the gloating and simplistic terms in which our newscasters "explain" what is happening. We need creative analysis, free from the conservative media's quick fix or the dogma that has sadly been so much a part of political discussion. Some, fearful of risking unfamiliar terrain, argue that what has happened in the Soviet Union and in Eastern Europe is simply part of the ongoing process of creating socialism. As the eternal optimist, I do not doubt it. But what is happening here, in the West, is also a part of that process—because, call it what you will, we humans must move towards a more humane and procreative form of society or we will destroy our habitat.

But can we write off the recent socialist setbacks simply as *part of the process?* Can we fail to consider them as real reverses that, although undoubtedly part of the process, also push that process back generations? We must search for the problem areas. Where were the most flagrant mistakes? What was left unattended? Where did the cracks occur? An honest and useful look requires that we challenge all the myths.

I believe that in each of the revolutionary experiments the failure to develop an indigenous feminist discourse and a vital feminist agenda impeded the consolidation that would push an otherwise more humane society forward. Again and always, the men had their way. It was obviously too frightening to have to confront the unleashed power of women, silenced for centuries. Easier to pay lip service to "women's rights," while being careful not to allow them to become a priority or to threaten male power. An important degree of stagnation set in perhaps—among other reasons—because *our very understanding of the relationship between base and superstructure was erroneous.* Perhaps the concept of *base* itself must be redefined.

Further, the limitations placed upon critical analysis blind us to the ways in which we continue to deceive ourselves. As Hubbard and others point out, patriarchal expectations and attitudes are so utterly embedded in how we view the world that each assessment or reassessment requires the courage to question even that which we hold as *knowledge*. Patriarchy profoundly affects how we see ourselves within the construct. A new look at the role of memory is essential here.

In the university, for example, we still talk about "women's history" and "women's literature," when our entire conception of history and literature is off because these disciplines have ignored women. Women's words have not been heard. In medicine, in law, in biology, in every field, our understanding is characterized by a lopsided male-centered vision. Building upon a crooked foundation, we have naturally not been able to construct a livable house.

Under capitalism, we are always up against a system whose viability is based upon our exploitation. In the revolutionary experiments, a responsible development of the theory and practice of changing human relationships has faced another kind of stress. As the struggle to emerge from poverty and dependence make daily life difficult, in whatever political context, people feel more acutely a deepening *loss of self*. This is a much more serious problem than the curtailment of travel, the unavailability of Levis, or the lack of variety in people's diet. Although not everyone would articulate the problem in the same way, affronts to cultural autonomy, consciousness, spirituality, spontaneity, sexuality, or individual freedoms take a tremendous toll.

Classic Marxist analysis still tends to understand social and political change primarily in economic terms. Economic relations were not developed as they should have been, the story goes, and thus the cave-ins. Although I would agree that in most of the socialist countries economic relations were far from socialist in nature, that worker control had often become a farce, and extreme centralization made production and distribution systems look like prehistoric beasts of burden—to say nothing of the ways in which the socialist economies were affected by capitalist hegemony—still I intuit and insist that these were not the only, nor perhaps even the major, problems. The failure to understand the importance of feminism, race relations, cultural diversity, sexual difference, critical thought, certain individual freedoms, and the nature of power itself, all had a role in tearing these experiments apart. People became disaffected and were ultimately unwilling to defend revolutions they could not feel a part of.

Of course this is hardly a new insight. Rosa Luxemburg's disagreement with Lenin's concept of the party came from her fears that it would become elitist, that unequal power relations and bureaucracy would inevitably set in when the so-called professional revolutionaries, rather than the workers themselves, controlled the means of production. Inevitably, a new class would gain privilege and misuse power. Raya Dunayevskaya took these ideas further. But today we have new tools, like feminist theory and feminist therapy, that permit us to make the connections between our capacity to see ourselves in society and the ways we construct our social order. The vision that reclaimed memory brings is essential to these connections. For women, whose memory has been robbed by a history of patriarchy, this is particularly important. In fact, it is important for all groups whose culture has been obscured, distorted, denied. The empowering force of people's culture is something the social scientists are just beginning to pay attention to.

Workers must control their labor. Women must come to know and control our lives. We must become center to ourselves and to society, not *other*. The development of a feminist discourse is necessary if we are to *take* the power that is not offered us. Feminist theory demystifies our lives. It shows us that only by looking at our reality and moving to alter it, will we be able to realize our full potential *as women, and therefore as human beings*.

Centuries of patriarchy have meant the use and abuse of women. Patriarchal attitudes continue to protect or obscure the violence routinely perpetrated against us. So many adult women have been victims of incest or other forms of childhood sexual abuse that we can legitimately speak of epidemic damage.

Feminist therapy, solidly rooted in the retrieval and re-evaluation of what was done to us as children, gives us the tools we need to heal the wounds, reconnect with our strength, empower our actions. For generations the Freudian myths perpetuated a false placement of responsibility: we imagined being invaded and used, we were "hysterical" for daring to suggest such things, we were confused because we were not believed and shamed because we "lied"—or told. Feminist therapy, in retrieving memory, alters knowledge. Our primary knowledge of self, and the self-esteem that comes along with it, is restored. We see the world differently when we see it from this centered place.

I want to make it clear that I am not advocating an

emphasis on a recovery that is *disconnected from political analysis*. The popular recovery movement is very much like all other commercially nurtured phenomena: it contains kernels of truth and innumerable examples of pseudo-theory that prey on people's vulnerability. My point is that personal wholeness and political health, too often considered antagonistic, must be rewoven into a single fabric. They cannot be separated.

Elayne Rapping argues against "the recovery movement . . . as a political philosophy," and sets healing ourselves and changing the world in opposition to each other.[4] I do not believe in such an opposition. Powerful interests are served, on both sides, by perpetuating the idea that political change must not take feelings into account, or that being in touch with our feelings or living an examined life has nothing to do with politics. Such ideas are patriarchal inventions.

The promotion and protection of certain individual freedoms may seem to contradict the collective good. But I think this principle has been seen too rigidly in most of the socialist systems. Basic to these freedoms is the freedom to repossess memory, to know ourselves. Another is the freedom to claim physical space, to move, travel, choose the place or succession of places we wish to inhabit. Both our place of origin and chosen place are essential to memory's work—for the individual and the community.

I am thinking here of the problems that arose when the Sandinistas moved numbers of Miskito villages away from the border during the years of contra war. The revolutionaries wanted to protect the people from enemy attack. For the Miskitos, the placement of their villages was above all cultural, including the graves of their ancestors. In their haste and ignorance, the Sandinistas protected a population from enemy attack but also inflicted wounds that are still healing, and that impeded a consolidation of the revolution itself.

But back to feminism. As long as the newer ideas and methodologies in feminist therapy are considered "bourgeois luxuries," as they were in most revolutionary societies, their liberating force was denied to women struggling to understand themselves. And travel: what would it have cost the Cuban Revolution if from the beginning it had allowed people the freedom to travel outside the country, visit relatives in other places, come and go as they wished? Nothing but a lesser level of discontent. In fact, the whole mystique connected with family visitation through Miami would have been greatly deflated. And those who chose not to return? Their houses and consumption could have been used by others; their absence would have been the absence of those who didn't want to be there, those who for the most part gave little and took much.

It seems the Cubans now agree, for as of 1991 anyone over the age of eighteen may leave the country and return, as long as the money for such trips comes from abroad. But I remember a time in the early 1970s when a Mexican friend married to a Cuban woman struggled doggedly with such restrictions. They lived for several years in Cuba and had a young daughter. They wanted to move to Mexico. He, particularly, wanted to return to his home in Veracruz. She refused to let the Cuban authorities force her into leaving "like a *gusano*."[5] She was a revolutionary woman and demanded her right to travel back and forth, to visit the grandparents of her child. This couple had to wait three years, until the revolution became convinced of their "seriousness." Finally, they got what they demanded. I marveled at how their relationship survived. Many were not so resolute, or so fortunate.

Other, perhaps even more essential, individual liberties include the freedom to question, the freedom to exercise a passion for analytical thought and creative expression, the freedom to search for one's roots with all the risks inherent in that, and the freedom to remember that which has been emotionally obscured. Again, I am referring here, among other issues, to our need to deal with childhood sexual abuse, memories of which are frequently blocked by the trauma itself. In the United States and other Western nations, several generations of women are now retrieving such memory and it is changing our lives.

Feminist theory and therapy have gone a long way towards unlocking the prison into which patriarchy and aspects of Freudian philosophy have imprisoned the female psyche. But generally speaking, as I've said, these new therapies have not been granted much space within the socialist experiments. They have been seen as bourgeois luxuries, or perhaps just not priorities. This is unfortunate, because changing society can be enormously stressful, and getting in touch with ourselves extremely helpful. The connections empower us at all levels of living and working. Because women have been written out of history, *and history has been written without us*, we must insist on the freedom to remember, recreate, and return to our centrality.

My interest throughout this book has been feminism and how I perceive twentieth-century revolutionary experiments failing to develop a feminist agenda within their own processes of change. Some of the reasons for this seem clear, others less so.

Under neither socialism nor capitalism are men interested in giving up privilege. Those with power never are. So when it's a question of building day-care centers so that children will be better cared for and women able to work, this has been possible even in some of the more humane of the capitalist societies (France, Canada, and the Scandinavian countries, to name a few). Of course there's the old struggle, which certainly took place in the early days of the Cuban Revolution, in which men told their wives: "You don't need to work; I'm perfectly capable of working for us both!" Oh, those words that women, conditioned to believe that our self-realization comes from successful allegiance to a man, await with such eagerness. Often we discover too late that they are a prison from which we may yet be able to fight our way free—but never without great personal costs to us and to those we love.

In the countries where economic conditions require that a family have more than a single income, governments are sometimes willing, at least on paper, to support the concept of children being cared for by institutions rather than by "naturally endowed" mothers. This frees both parents to work outside the home. In these times of worldwide economic recession, under socialism as well as capitalism, the single-income family is becoming a luxury.

When women demand equal access to education, equal pay for equal work, and protective legislation, socialist revolutions—in contrast with capitalist societies—have been willing to fight for these changes. Capitalism, whose survival depends upon keeping women and other groups as reserve labor, cannot permit too much equality.

We get into much cloudier areas when we talk about abortion and other reproductive rights. Here we must contend with the power of patriarchal concepts of ownership and religion, especially in places like Nicaragua (and Louisiana!) where there is a deeply Catholic tradition. It's interesting to note that a woman's right to choose abortion is now under particular attack in the United States, where fundamentalism is doing patriarchy's dirty work. The issue of reproduction and who controls it always goes to the heart of male control.

Power remains a major problem. When, year after year, only a few token women are elected to positions of political power, socialism seems to defeat its purpose: that of creating a more just society for all people. The process of women acquiring political power in the Soviet Union and most of Eastern Europe was particularly slow, so slow as to remain ludicrous; it was more successful in Vietnam, Nicaragua, and Cuba. But nowhere in the socialist world has women's representation at the highest levels grown beyond tokenism, and, more to the point, women with a feminist vision have systematically been denied positions of power.

A seriously inhibiting challenge to feminism—and to socialism!—is the fact that almost all socialist experiments to date have accepted the nuclear family structure without question, assuming it is the best or most "natural" of human relations. And so the struggles around unpaid reproduction and upkeep (housework, the buying and preparation of food, attention to the husband's daily needs, child care, etc.), as well as those around gay and lesbian rights, have played themselves out in the most traditional arenas. The husband, wife, and offspring are seen as the core unit. The economy is based on the reproduction of this unit.

The needs of lesbians, or heterosexual women who choose to be single, are considered, if at all, in some sort of separate (unequal) sphere. Men who choose single lives are never so stigmatized, unless they are gay and choose to assume their sexual orientation publicly, in which case—depending upon the degree of homophobia in a given culture—they will also be considered *other*. Women are especially vulnerable because men believe they own us, and through us our offspring. This is one of the reasons that heterosexism is so limiting to the healing and growth of society as a whole.

Even under socialism, the issues raised by authentic feminist discourse have rarely been permitted to surface. Where they have surfaced, they have quickly been repressed in the struggle for "broader" objectives. In the industrialized nations, because there is a higher level of production and education, both of which provide more leisure for discussion and greater possibility for experimentation by the elite, feminist issues have emerged more explicitly. But they are so marginal to the arenas of power and accessible to so few women as to be practically irrelevant.

What about the effects of gender bias and sexism on centuries of tradition? Or, as Adrienne Rich so aptly labels it, compulsory heterosexuality?[6] How has humankind's understanding of history—of knowledge itself—been damaged? What distortions do we inherit that inevitably affect the choices we make, including those we make when we set out to change society?

How can women know our power if we do not know our history, if we cannot retrieve our memory, if we cannot occupy our own centrality, and if society is denied our vision? What is lost to leadership when we cannot reap the benefits of women's ways of seeing, knowing, and valuing? What social distortions and conditioning continue to be perpetrated? What of the blind eye that society still turns toward violence against women in all of its manifestations, its acceptance of images which portray women as objects of male desire, its acquiescence to women's role as caretakers, servicers, helpmates?

When a political system, be it socialist or capitalist, rewards women for having or not having children, or attempts to control our reproductive choices, when it rewards us for patience, endurance, submission, silence—what does this inevitably mean in the lives of future generations of females and males? For an imme-

diate take on how sexist and misogynist values are perpetuated in a given society, one need only look at images of women and the roles we are assigned: in school
texts from the earliest grades, in advertising, and in the
media. No revolutionary rhetoric in the world can compete with the take-home messages transmitted by this
continuous conditioning.

There is no question in my mind that a revolutionary
movement, in or out of power, unable to address the
needs of women, people of color, or any other group,
will have a very hard time dealing with those needs in
the society it envisions or constructs. If a revolution is
unable or unwilling to address the needs of *all* people,
it is doomed to failure. The idea of a revolution within
the revolution, as proclaimed in the Cuban experience,
will inevitably keep the first in the shadow of the
second. It's the difference between understanding
feminism as an isolated piece or as integral to struggle,
as one of the motors of social change.

What other questions can we ask? One is how
memory and power are related. Authentic power comes
from a fully developed sense of self, possible only when
both individual and collective memory is retrieved.
Patriarchy has effectively erased women's memory,
making it extremely difficult for us to connect with our
history, learn from our foremothers, know who we are.
How can we hope to see ourselves as anything but *other*
when our identity is distorted, our needs continue to be
secondary, and men usurp our decision-making process?
How can we redefine power, for ourselves and for
society?

What kind of world do we want?

How can we achieve it?

We do not need to wonder about the difference feminism makes in women's lives. Our own experience tells us it is definitive. For those of us who have come to a lesbian identity, or have always known we were lesbians, a feminist theoretical framework is not automatic, but it is logical. Again, in the context of this discussion I speak not only of individual lesbian women, but of lesbianism as an option that challenges so much of what patriarchy is about.

For those women who *choose* heterosexuality, a vision that gives us back ourselves is equally essential. The paradox here is that for the vast majority it cannot be a choice until compulsory heterosexuality is not our social mode. Heterosexual women must deal, in their intimate lives, with men who are threatened with loss of privilege, and this too is a struggle worth waging.

We may well wonder what difference a feminist world view could make to society, since we have no modern models. Some theorists believe in an inherent (or biological) female essence which, were women in power, would place technology at the service of life, ecological sanity, and peace. I myself am not such a biological determinist. I know that race, class, culture, and other pieces of the puzzle must be factored in along with gender to create the total picture. Creative analysis of a particular situation may tell us that one of these pieces is particularly important to the struggle being waged: for example, class in the early union battles, the preservation of culture to Native American peoples, or race, historically and today.[7]

Throughout, a male way of seeing has dominated, depriving us all of a vision that has been ignored or disempowered. I don't believe we yet possess a broad view of how a true honoring of womanness might change our lives.

For men, the development of a feminist discourse also returns a missing piece. For we are first of all human. Whoever denies humanity to others loses a part of his own. The historical experiences of the slave owner, the conqueror, the prison warden, may all be referenced here. It is not easy to give up privilege, but it is possible. And ultimately liberating.

When we talk about the intersection of class, race, gender, sexuality, age, physical and mental ability, and other variables, we must demand for gender the same ongoing analysis that we demand for class and race. It is not a matter of adding on. The problem is qualitative, calling forth a vision that does not relegate half of humanity as *other*, but rather thoroughly reassesses a world view and a view of history itself.

In thinking about the issues outlined here, I continually wonder *how* I lost the self-knowledge that might have empowered me to ask these questions from my woman-centered identity instead of accepting the male line that repeatedly urged me to put aside my own needs in the struggle for social change. What, exactly, was the process?

It's easy enough to point to the signs and symbols, the myths that surround us, causing us to lose our balance long before our birth. But I am always searching for the personal, visceral, process—how it moves within my body, changing me. It never *felt* right to submit, to cede. Yet I did so for a very long time. Still do, in pieces. And again, not *why* I did this, but—literally—*how*. The *why* is what patriarchy is about; the *how* is process.

A personal story may have relevance. By telling it, I do not wish to isolate or place undue emphasis upon my particular experience. I want to point to the hidden links between the personal and the political, where we find that cause and effect are often connected in non-linear ways. These are the lessons of our lives.

In the context of psychotherapy, I have recently had some insights into this question. For a number of years I have been working on confronting a phobia that comes from having been sexually abused as a young child, and I find myself repeatedly formulating the work in terms of *should*: "I *should* try harder to deal with this . . . ." The element of choice seems tellingly absent. Some of my missing pieces, in the form of vivid memories recalled while under hypnosis, bring with them the understanding that I will not be able to confront my fear until I get rid of the *should*, until I can make conscious choices at each juncture.

I remember one of my abusers, my maternal grandfather who was a religious authority as well as the family patriarch, raping me and then saying: "Be a good girl. You'll be a good girl now, won't you?" The rhetorical question was a stand-in for don't tell. And for a long long time I didn't tell.

I did not rebel. Like so many others, I protected my

abuser by keeping his secret: not in response to further torture or even threats, but simply because he told me to *be good*. It was enough. And throughout too much of the rest of my life I had only to hear those words, or some variation of them, and I was sure to follow orders: *Be good. Accept the line. Obey authority.*

Under patriarchy, in different ways and with varying degrees of coercion and force, women are taught from an early age to acquiesce. To accept authority. Not to ask the difficult questions, even when something *feels* wrong. Perhaps especially when something feels wrong. Feelings, after all, are suspect. We are to understand that success is only accountable to male reason.

We women who believe in a world in which it is possible to live and work and love and raise our children, we women who *demand* ecological sanity and peace, who know that creativity is change, who no longer accept the promises and the crumbs: what can we do? In what directions must we move? Certainly it is necessary to reject the linear dogmas that continuous-ly confront us with false dichotomies: between politics and spirituality, reason and feeling, mind and body. We must develop new theories and strategies, born of a circular or spiral way of knowing, rather than the lifeless line that has led us nowhere but into the service of our own worst interests.

Feminist theory, therapy, and practice lay bare the abusive mechanisms and empower us to re-member, to reclaim and trust our experiences, to defy authority in whatever form, and to challenge ideologies that main-tain us as *other*. I do not believe that emotional wounds alone are responsible for women's willingness—and sometimes eagerness—to remain dependent upon ways of knowing and of acting that betray our deepest needs. Certainly class oppression compounds this, as well as race, age, affectational orientation, and other variables.

But we must reassemble the many subtle, and not so subtle, often overlapping ways in which the distortion of our personal and collective histories has prevented us from living in and with ourselves. We must reach back through women's stories, to reconstruct memory and connection. In whatever political system, we must develop a discourse that centers us in our lives and in the world. Socialist society, or a society whose goal is a decent and meaningful life for everyone, has a much greater possibility of providing the space for radical change. What is needed is the willingness to risk, to maintain a healthy courage, and to understand that by promoting autonomy change itself may be more permanent.

# NOTES

## TO SET A CONTEXT

1. "The Master's Tools Will Never Dismantle the Master's House," 1979.

2. Interview in *La mujer nicaragüense en los años 80* ("Nicaraguan Women in the 1980s"), by Ada Julia Brenes et al. (Managua: Ediciones Nicarao, 1991).

## CHAPTER 1

1. *La boletina* is the bimonthly publication of *Puntos de Encuentro*, Apartado Postal RP-39, Managua, Nicaragua. It is a feminist publication representing the current thoughts and actions of a whole new generation of Nicaraguan women. This quote is from the editorial in no. 1, November-December 1991.

2. The Sandinista National Liberation Front (FSLN) was founded in 1961 by Carlos Fonseca, Tomás Borge, and several other young Nicaraguan revolutionaries. Some came from the ranks of the Nicaraguan Socialist Party, some were students, all looked to Augusto C. Sandino, anti-imperialist hero of the 1920s and 1930s, as their revolutionary mentor. With few exceptions, early women in the FSLN were girlfriends and sisters of the male members, and then young women from the Christian movement who also envisioned a different Nicaragua and had tired of the more traditionalist routes. As the organization developed through the late 1960s and early 1970s, women joined in greater numbers; and many came to occupy leadership roles.

3. Augusto C. Sandino, revolutionary leader of the 1920s and 1930s. Nicaraguan poet and sculptor Ernesto Cardenal designed the fifteen-story

statue, raised at the highest point in the capital city shortly before the current government took office. It was illuminated by two vertical strings of light back then, but after the conservative victory the electricity was cut off. Still, the figure remains on army land controlled by the Sandinistas. Its presence reflects both continuance and challenge.

4. The First Congress's "Resolution on the Situation of Nicaraguan Women" begins: "The FSLN recognizes the participation and determination of Nicaraguan women in the economic, social, and political demands achieved during these difficult years of our people's struggle. In this process, women have made important gains; nevertheless, in spite of their high level of participation, situations of discrimination remain in different areas of their life, in the public sphere as well as in the home. At the present time this discrimination has worsened due to an absence of specific women's rights policies on the part of the current government. Women are in an even more vulnerable position because of the economic and social measures which this government has adopted in its effort to destroy the gains of the revolution." The resolution goes on to enumerate a series of points which will guide future attention to women's issues. These include an emphasis on ideological work among members of the FSLN, continued defense of those gains made over the past eleven years, and the establishment of a special commission to increase the number of women at all levels of party leadership. The congress recognized the existence of a double moral standard as regards female and male members of the party, and pledged itself to continue fighting sexism in its ranks and to strengthen the organization of women in the countryside and cities, farming cooperatives, unions, and other entities where a gender-conscious participation may be possible; to see maternity as a social rather than an individual responsibility, and to encourage men to share in this social responsibility; and to struggle against all expressions of sexism within the Party as well as in society as a whole. The resolution defined sexism as "a retrograde residual ideology, unacceptable for revolutionaries."

5. Dora María Téllez was a medical student from a upper-middle-class family who went underground with the FSLN in the mid-1970s. At twenty-two, she was third in command of the spectacular takeover of the National Palace in 1978. A year later she and her mostly female high command took the city of León, facilitating the establishment of the first revolutionary government which would take definitive control of the country in July 1979. During the ten years of Sandinista government, Téllez was minister of public health and vice president of the Council of

State, among other important positions. Today she is still a member of the legislative body (voted into office in the 1990 elections). In that arena she fights alongside other revolutionaries to safeguard what ten years of Sandinismo was able to accomplish.

6. The conference put forth the concept of reciprocal solidarity, which would transform the international solidarity movement from its role as object to subject. Activists from across the world discussed the need to build more political relationships with the FSLN. Concretely, projects should be designed to benefit and advance the struggles of both countries. In this context, the U.S. Nicaraguan Network proposed to assist the FSLN in deepening the process of feminist consciouness-raising within the party, beginning with but not exclusive to women.

7. The Luisa Amanda Espinosa Nicaraguan Women's Association (AMNLAE) is the continuation of the Organization of Nicaraguan Women Confronting the Problems of the Nation (AMPRONAC), a group founded by the FSLN during the last years of the war against Somoza. It is the FSLN's female arm. Although it went through a number of changes during the ten years of Sandinista government, it remains under party leadership. Luisa Amanda Espinosa, whose name the organization bears, was the first woman to die in the guerrilla struggle which began in the 1960s.

8. Since Michele Costa was the Nicaragua Network's outgoing coordinator, soon to be replaced by Kathy Hoyt de González, Kathy was also present at this meeting. So was Magda Enríquez, the FSLN's representative in the United States.

9. *Feminist Theory: From Margin to Center* (Boston: South End, 1984), p. 194.

10. June Jordan, "A New Politics of Sexuality," "Just Inside the Door," her bimonthly column for *The Progressive*, 12 July 1991.

11. Raya Dunayevskaya (1910-1987), to quote Adrienne Rich's new forward to her classic *Rosa Luxemburg, Women's Liberation, and Marx's Philosophy of Revolution* (Champaign, Ill.: University of Illinois Press, 1991), "was a major thinker in the history of Marxism and of women's liberation—one of the longest continuously active woman revolutionaries of the twentieth century." She was born in a border town in the Ukraine, but came to the United States at the age of 13 where she worked with black activists in Chicago, with West Virginia miners on strike in 1949-1950, and later deeply involved herself with the women's liberation movement that emerged in the mid-1960s. She conceived of

women not only as a force but as a "revolutionary reason." Dunayevskaya became Trotsky's Russian-language secretary in 1937, during his exile in Mexico, but broke with him two years later because he continued to believe that the Soviet system contained the seeds of communism and she saw it as a state-capitalist society, proposing as well that state-capitalism was a new world stage. In her many books she examines issues of organization, power, values, the relationship between base and superstructure, and what happens after a revolutionary movement comes to power (questions that continue to have enormous relevance). Wayne State University Archives of Labor and Urban Affairs issued *Marxist-Humanism: A Half-Century of Its World Development*, more than 15,000 pages of her work available on microfilm. Of particular interest to feminists, besides the above-cited book on Luxemburg, is her *Women's Liberation and the Dialectics of Revolution: Reaching for the Future* (Atlantic Highlands, NJ: Humanities Press International), currently out of print.

12. I am thinking particularly of Audre Lorde, Gloria Anzaldua, Adrienne Rich, Blanche Wiesen Cook, bell hooks, June Jordan, and others.

## CHAPTER 2

1. Interview with the author, *Sandino's Daughters* (Vancouver: New Star Books, 1981), p. 56.

2. Doris Tijerino, *Inside the Nicaraguan Revolution* (Vancouver: New Star Books, 1978), *Sandino's Daughters: Conversations With Nicaraguan Women in Struggle* (Vancouver: New Star Books, 1981), plus numerous contributions to other books, essays, and articles.

3. UNO stands for National Union of the Opposition, a coalition of fourteen conservative and centrist political parties brought together under the Bush administration's plan to oust the Sandinistas. UNO's presidential candidate was Violeta Barrios de Chamorro, the widow of a beloved liberal politician who was murdered in 1978 during the war against Somoza.

4. AMPRONAC, Asociacion de Mujeres ante la Problematica Nacional (Association of Women Confronting the Problems of the Nation). This women's organization, the predecessor to AMNLAE, was mainly

promoted by the leadership of what would become the FSLN's proletarian tendency, one of the three groups into which the movement split in the mid-1970s, only to unify itself again in 1978.

5. Luisa Amanda Espinosa (1948-1970) was a young working-class woman, one of twenty-one sisters and brothers. Interviews I conducted with family and friends during my fieldwork for *Sandino's Daughters* led me to believe that she suffered personal childhood abuse as well as extreme poverty. She joined the FSLN at an early age, and is believed to have been the first female member of the organization killed in battle. On April 3, 1970, she and a male comrade were discovered in a safe house and she may have been unarmed when she went down. After the war it was decided that the FSLN's women's organization should bear her name.

6. This and much of the information that follows is from "Construcción de la democracia en Nicaragua" ("Building Democracy in Nicaragua"), by Ana Criquillion (Managua: Editorial UCA, 1988).

7. In a sixty-day period from the Sandinista's electoral defeat to the new government's installation, a revolutionary party that ten years before had literally moved from guerrilla warfare to positions of state power was now faced with legitimizing the living situations of many of its leadership. Most of the highest FSLN officials were still living in mansions abandoned by the bourgeoisie. Their small salaries and lack of stipends or graft had made it impossible for them to buy land, homes, and automobiles. Compared to members of other governments, their lives were, indeed, frugal. Many also had not been thinking ahead to a time when they might no longer be in power. For this reason, the FSLN pushed through a law permitting the legalization of a certain amount of personal property. A few Sandinista leaders abused this law, signing over to themselves or relatives and friends more than was necessary. In poverty-stricken Nicaragua the scandal, referred to as the *piñata* (a decorated clay pot at a birthday or other holiday that is tapped by a group of blindfolded children, producing a rain of toys and sweets) was uncovered and rectified. The practice was neither widespread nor indicative of the party as a whole. But the right continues to point to the *piñata* as a sign of corruption in the FSLN.

8. Sylvia Saakes, "Particularidades del movimiento de mujeres en Nicaragua bajo el gobierno sandinista" ("Particularities of the Nicaraguan Women's Movement Under the Sandinista Government"), *La mujer nicaragüense en los años 80* ("Nicaraguan Women in the Eighties") (Managua: Ediciones Nicarao, 1991), p. 177.

9. At least 7.5 million, although new research is bringing to light additional data. (Sources include *Barricada International*, the Inter-hemispheric Resource Center in Albuquerque, New Mexico, and *The Guardian* newspaper in New York.)

10. The male members of the Somoza family had dictatorial control of Nicaragua for almost half a century. It represented a literal reign of terror, with extreme repression of whole sectors of the population, imprisonment of anyone in the opposition, and frequent cases of torture. The outright murder of many progressive students led some to say that during the Somoza regime it was a crime to be young. The Somozas always enjoyed the support of the United States. They owned so much land and business in the country that when the FSLN took power in 1979 it simply nationalized what belonged to them, and land reform was well underway. The deposed Somoza took refuge first in Miami and then in Paraguay, where a commando of Argentine revolutionaries was able to eliminate him a couple of years later.

11. Wilhelm Reich was a disciple of Freud and a member of the Austrian Communist Party. His most important work examines the changes in sexual politics during the first years of the Russian Revolution, the links between authoritarian family structure and people's willingness to support authoritarian social systems, and the ways in which inhibited emotional life breeds sick human beings. Reich was expelled from the CP, and later immigrated to the United States where he acquired a fairly large following. Eventually, he was also persecuted by the U.S. government. He became paranoid toward the end of his life. More about Reich later on. In the 1980s, Alice Miller, another ex-disciple of Freud, began publishing her major works: *Drama of the Gifted Child, Thou Shalt Not be Aware,* and *Breaking Down the Walls of Silence*. Miller not only broke with those theories of Freud's that have kept women out of touch with themselves for so long, she also broke with psychoanalysis. Among the theorists who have made important connections between patriarchal abuse and the way women perceive themselves in the world, Miller opens some essential doors.

12. "Discusión entre mujeres: El fantasma del 52% recorre Nicaragua" ("Discussion Among Women: The Phantom of the 52% Majority Sweeps Nicaragua"), *El Nuevo Diario*, 17 October 1991.

13. "AMNLAE denuncia peligrosa campaña" ("AMNLAE Denounces Dangerous Campaign"), *El Nuevo Diario*, Managua, 9 October 1991.

14. "Risposta a AMNLAE" ("Response to AMNLAE"), signed by Luz

Marina Tórrez, Bertha Inés Cabrales, and Nora Meneses, *El Nuevo Diario*, Managua, 13 October 1991.

15. "Discusión entre mujeres."

16. This and further quotes are from Julie Light's article, "Women's Confab Turnout Elates Managua Feminists," *The Guardian*, 5 February 1992.

17. Final statement of the meeting of Nicaraguan women, "Unity in Diversity," translation and emphasis mine.

18. *Barricada International* 12, no. 349 (May 1992).

19. Ibid.

20. This and following quotes are from my conversation with Ana, Amy, Hazel, Mary, and Carmen, in Managua, 17 October 1991.

21. A brigade of lesbians and gay men from San Francisco who came to build a community center in the Managua neighborhood of Selim Shible, generally considered to have been the beginning of organized ties between gays and lesbians in the United States and Nicaragua.

22. Gay Pride Day commemorates the June 27, 1969, Stonewall Rebellion in New York City, where for the first time customers at a Puerto Rican gay bar resisted police harassment. It was a lesbian who first refused arrest and sparked two days of street fighting in which 400 of New York City's "finest" were confronted by more than 2,000 homosexuals. More than any other event, Stonewall marked the birth of gay and lesbian movements worldwide. Gay Pride was celebrated in Latin America for the first time in 1979, in Mexico City. The first Nicaraguan celebration was in 1991.

23. *El Nuevo Diaro*, 1, 2, and 3 July 1991; *Barricada*, 2 July 1991; *Gente*, 5 July 1991.

24. In Nicaragua, and Latin America in general, the word homosexual is used to refer to gay men.

25. This is an internationally important center of film study, founded by Cubans in conjunction with Colombian Nobel Prize winning novelist Gabriel García Márquez. Students come from all over Latin America and the world. Cuba's film industry, itself outstanding, has had an interesting history. It was built to early importance by an old communist and gay man named Alfredo Guevara. Brilliant, innovative, one of the country's most creative forces, Guevara was suddenly removed from his post at the head of the Cuban Film Institute (ICAIC, Cuban Institute of Film, Art and Industry) in the late-1970s and named ambassador to France. Recently

he was reinstated as ICAIC's director and at the Cuban Communist Party's Fourth Congress in October 1991 he was elevated to the party's Central Committee.

26. In June 1991, Nicaragua's National Assembly voted 43 to 41 to pass Article No. 205 of the Penel Code, an anti-sodomy law punishing homosexuality between consenting adults with up to three years in prison. The thirty-seven Sandinista delegates present all voted against the article as did several others. There has been enormous protest, but the article became law in July. This was a severe blow to gay activism and to overall human rights in Nicaragua.

27. The first wave of feminism was the nineteenth-century women's rights movement which emerged primarily in the United States and England. It concerned itself with issues of legal autonomy, property, conditions and wages in the work place, the abolition of slavery, the demand for suffrage, and peace. The issue of race frequently divided the movement. Feminism re-emerged in the 1960s, again particularly in the industrialized nations. Building upon the pioneering work of our sisters a century before, this second wave defined feminism in terms of a world view—reproductive rights and other health concerns, different sexual orientations, and the retrieval of memory have been added to a multiple agenda. Again, race and class have often divided the ranks, as middle-class white women exercise the luxury of a polemic which few working-class women, or women of color, have. On the other hand, by now the gains of the feminist movement affects society in general and the movement has become more truly international—today black, Latina, and other "minority" women throughout the world are at the forefront of feminist discourse and action.

28. Figures are from "Feminization of Poverty?" *Barricada International* 11, no. 341 (September 1991): 19-21.

29. It is often pointed out that each succeeding revolutionary experience incorporates more women into its process. In El Salvador, for example, the FMLN (Farabundo Martí National Liberation Front) adopted regulations governing percentages of women among the leadership at local, regional, and national levels. At least at the lower levels, 50 percent of that leadership had to be female.

30. Ernesto "Che" Guevara was an Argentine doctor who met Cuban revolutionaries in Guatemala in 1954 and later became one of the central figures in the Cuban revolutionary struggle. After the victory in 1959, he was minister of heavy industry and president of the National Bank,

among other positions. In 1964 he disappeared from the Cuban scene to fulfill what he saw as his personal/political destiny: to continue making revolution elsewhere. He died fighting for the liberation of Latin America in Bolivia in October 1967. His murder, without trial, was ordered by the CIA.

## CHAPTER 3

1. Enid Dame, "Ethel Rosenberg: A Sestina," in *Anything You Don't See* (Albuquerque: West End Press, 1991).

2. While writing this book, I preferred to wait before characterizing the decline of European socialism as anything but apparent. On the one hand, what developed in the Soviet Union and the countries within its immediate sphere of influence had clearly become corrupted. I'm not sure we can call it socialism. On the other, recent and increasing protests by people in Russia, Poland, and elsewhere tell us that the desire for socialism is far from dead. Certainly the experience obtained throughout the past seventy years and by so many different peoples are not lost in the forms of political organization that are taking the place of what we once called socialism.

3. An article in the *Albuquerque Journal,* 24 May 1992, suggests there has been a change in the wording of Pentagon policy documents. Whereas they formerly made it very clear that competitive power would not be tolerated from any other country, now they use phrases such as "democracies coexisting with one another."

4. The organization of society itself tends to protect the prevalence of violence against women: in the home, in schools and work places, and on the streets. Great numbers of women are battered within their families, yet choose to remain in a victimized position because they are not believed, can visualize no alternative, have come to accept this as "natural," or otherwise see no way out. We now know that abuse is widespread, that it crosses all class and racial lines, and that women often suffer what is known as battered women's syndrome, becoming so fearful of losing their small turf that they repeatedly protect and return to their batterer. Often it is too late, and they are murdered by abusive husbands who had made promises to change. Or, they themselves are pushed to kill their batterer. In the United States, many women are

serving long prison terms for this crime of self-defense. Robin Morgan writes: "Because of the courage of average women, high-profile personalities now dare to speak out on having survived battery ('Miss America' Carolyn Sapp), child abuse (Roseanne Barr, LaToya Jackson, Sinead O'Connor), sexual harassment (Anita Hill)." *Ms.* 2, no. 3 (November/December 1991): 1.

5. See *The Pedagogy of the Oppressed* and other books by Freire, who is a Brazilian theoretician and practitioner of popular education.

6. Cathy Porter's introduction to her translation of the novel *A Great Love* by Alexandra Kollontai (New York: Norton, 1981) makes a strong case for the married Lenin having had an affair with Ines Armand, a French revolutionary woman. Whether or not this was so, what is clear, is Kollontai's concern with the frequency with which male leaders subdue women who also show leadership qualities, placing their own needs above the women's possibilities for full creative work. Kollontai herself had suffered such a relationship with the Russian economist Maslov. And, through her friendship with Armand, she may indeed have been privy to that woman's similar situation with Lenin. In *A Great Love*, many years before "its time had come," Kollontai relentlessly explores a situation in which the revolutionary woman's loyalty to a male leader's emotional control and exploitation smothers her enthusiasm for struggle and for life, quite literally killing her "great love" for him. There is no conclusive proof, of the type that patriarchy demands, for the fact that Lenin had these personal attitudes or engaged in this type of behavior. On the other hand, Kollontai's not so subtle story makes me wonder. Certainly this double standard would have been common to men then, as it is today.

7. See especially Kollontai's "Towards a History of the Working Women's Movement in Russia," "The Social Basis of the Woman Question," "Theses on Communist Morality in the Sphere of Marital Relations," and "Sexual Relations and the Class Struggle," in *Selected Writings* (New York: Norton, 1977), Raya Dunayevskaya's *Rosa Luxemburg, Women's Liberation, and Marx's Philosophy of Revolution* (Atlantic Highlands, NJ: Humanities Press, 1981), and Wilhelm Reich, *The Sexual Revolution, The Function of the Orgasm*, and *The Mass Psychology of Fascism*.

8. Dunayevskaya, *Marxism and Freedom* (2nd ed., p. 17), as quoted by Adrienne Rich in her forward to the 1991 University of Illinois reissue of *Rosa Luxemburg, Women's Liberation, and Marx's Philosophy of Revolution*.

9. As explained in the first of Dunayevskaya's trilogy on revolution, *Marxism and Freedom, From 1776 Until Today,* 1958.

10. Dunayevskaya, *Rosa Luxemburg, Women's Liberation, and Marx's Philosophy of Revolution.*

11. Ibid., pp. xiv-xviii.

12. Ibid., p. 190.

13. Ibid., pp. 190-91.

14. Alexandra Kollontai, *Selected Writings,* with an introduction by Alix Holt (New York: Norton, 1977).

15. "USSR: It was the women . . . ," *Ms.* 2, no. 3 (November-December 1991): 14-15.

16. Slavenka Draculić, *How We Survived Communism and Even Laughed* (New York: Norton, 1992).

17. Quoted in Erika Monk's review of *How We Survived Communism and Even Laughed, The Women's Review of Books* 9, no. 8 (May 1992): 1.

18. Nicaragua, under the FSLN government, initiated a program that combined socialist, Christian, and Sandinista thought (attributed to Augusto C. Sandino). Although a mixed economy and political pluralism were always part of the Sandinista project, the U.S. media insisted on labeling Nicaragua's revolutionary government "socialist" and even "communist." What they really feared, I believe, was a project in which the traditional antagonism between Marxism and Christianity would break down and non-Christian and Christian revolutionaries realize they were struggling for similar goals. Throughout predominantly Catholic Latin America, this unity, indeed, poses a threat to continued U.S. domination.

19. We may want to make a distinction between using women's bodies in some cultural manifestation and using them in advertising that is commercial in nature, such as selling a product. The former may be art. In the latter case, body or bodily parts become particularly objectivized. In "Advertising Suit Over Sex in Beer Ads Comes as Genre Changes," Stuart Elliott in *The New York Times,* 12 November 1991, describes how women workers at the Stroh Brewery Company have filed a lawsuit linking increased sexual harassment on the job with the atmosphere created by the brewery's advertising campaign that featured young women in bikinis serving beer to a group of men. Not only female bodies,

but other sexual coding is frequent in sales pitches. A recent Coors TV commercial flashes four upside down pink triangles on the screen, symbol of the gay and lesbian lifestyle. As these triangles appear, almost subliminally, the trim young bodies of men as well as women link Coors to the idea of keeping fit. Superimposed over the last triangle are the words "the only shape to be in." I find this commercial particularly interesting in light of the fact that Coors has traditionally discriminated against gays, lesbians, and people of color. This example of subliminal advertising may be in response to successful boycotting by the gay, black, and Latina communities.

20. U.S. feminist historian Ruth Rosen reports on this meeting, first in a letter circulated to friends and then in an article in *Dissent*. The following quotes are from her letter.

21. *Cuban Women Now* (Toronto: The Women's Press, 1974), *Afterward* (Toronto: The Women's Press, 1974), *Cuban Women Twenty Years Later* (New York: Smyrna, 1981), and *Breaking the Silences: 20th Century Poetry by Cuban Women* (Vancouver: Pulp Press, 1982).

22. *Spirit of the People* (Vancouver: New Star Books, 1975).

# CHAPTER 4

1. Haydée Santamaría, heroine of Moncada, was a member of the Central Committee of the Cuban Communist Party, a member of the Council of State, and director of the Casa de las Américas, an important Cuban cultural institution, until she committed suicide in 1980. This quote is from a 1979 issue of *Granma*, the official Cuban Communist Party newspaper, Havana.

2. Before the break up of the Eastern bloc, 85 percent of Cuba's trade was with the socialist countries, 10 percent with the industrialized capitalist countries, and 5 percent with the so-called underdeveloped world. Today there is 15 percent less trade with Eastern Europe, and the Soviet Union has revoked Cuba's preferred-nation status. That country has also reduced its shipments of oil by 25 percent, from 13 to 10 million barrels a year. Contrary to what we read in the U.S. press, however, Soviet trade with Cuba continues and is not a one-way street. The Soviets buy 25 percent of all Cuban sugar, 40 percent of its citrus fruits, and 30 percent

of its nickel. Cuba currently sells $80 million worth of medical equipment and medicine a year to the Soviet Union. (Data from Cuban delegation to FSLN solidarity conference, Managua, Nicaragua, October 1991.)

3. Data from Cuban delegation to FSLN solidarity conference, Managua, Nicaragua, October 1991.

4. The Cuban Committees for the Defense of the Revolution (CDR) are voluntary block organizations, to which most neighbors belong. Common tasks include patrolling the streets against crime and counterrevolutionary attack, community cleanup and beautification programs, recycling, preventative medicine campaigns (such as registering women for free pap smears), blood drives, study circles and other activities that mobilize people to work together for social change.

5. I left the United States in 1961, accompanied by my son who was ten months old at the time. We lived in Mexico until 1969, where my three daughters were born. From 1969 to 1980 we lived in Cuba, and then two of my daughters and I moved to Nicaragua. Early in 1984, I returned to the United States.

6. Letter from Vikki Dow and Sonja de Vries, in the "Community Voices" column of *Gay Community News*, Boston, May 9-21, 1992.

7. Up to and including the 1970s, there were almost no female directors in the Cuban film industry; at least none who were making feature-length productions. Sara Gómez had been the lone exception, and in fact she was shooting a picture that dealt with feminist issues when she died suddenly of asthma. More than a decade passed before some of her male comrades in the industry completed the film. Gradually, a few women began making documentaries. By the 1980s a couple of female film makers joined the ranks of the still essentially male Cuban Institute of Film Art and Industry (ICAIC).

8. I am thinking particularly of the work of the Brazilian Vania Banbirra and the French-Chilean Michelle Mattalart.

9. The centerpiece of a speech by Fidel Castro to a meeting of Cuban artists in 1962. It has been quoted and used to bolster their arguments both by defenders and critics of the Cuban process.

10. For a moving look at how critics, dissidents, intellectuals, and artists fared under Stalinism in the Soviet Union, see Nadezhada Mandelstam's detailed account in *Hope Against Hope: A Memoir* (New York: Athenaeum, 1970).

11. Voice of America, Radio Free Europe, and more recently (with regard

to Cuba), Radio and TV Martí, urge defection and mass exodus by painting a Hollywood-like picture of life in the United States. This encourages many to come to this country by any means necessary: from legal visas to the periodic rushes of embassies and/or fleets of rickety over-filled boats. With utter disregard for human lives, and depending upon the political policy of the moment, the U.S. Immigration and Naturalization Service either admits or rejects these would-be immigrants. Eleven years after the 1980 Mariel exodus, hundreds of those who risked their lives to travel to the United States are still being kept in U.S. prisons and detention camps.

12. Critics of a revolutionary process are quick to generalize with isolated examples. Haydée Santamaría was an extraordinary woman, an early comrade of Castro, someone who had occupied many leadership positions within the Cuban process. She had also been imprisoned during the struggle against Batista, when her captors brought her lover's testicles and brother's eye to her in an unsuccessful attempt to break her spirit. She lived her brilliant and creative life on the psychological edge, and committed suicide in 1980. Oswaldo Dorticós, president of the republic, was terminally ill and took his life a few years later. Although two among hundreds of Cuban revolutionary leaders, using them as examples to generalize a state of discontent seem specious at best.

13. Name given to those who left Cuba in 1980 through the seaport of Mariel.

14. Fidel Castro, speech at Revolution Square, Havana, December 22, 1975.

15. It is estimated that the U.S. blockade, over a period of almost three decades, has cost the Cuban economy more than $15 billion. Cuba had come to depend upon the Soviet Union and the countries of Eastern Europe for 86.3 percent of its foreign trade. "Cuba navega con la historia" ("Cuba in Tune with History"), *Punto Final* (Santiago de Chile), no. 250 (November 1991): 14-15.

16. From *Current History*, no. 3 (1991), quoted in "Las posibilidades de vencer" ("The Possibilities of Victory") *Punto Final*, no. 250 (November 1991): 15. Gunn points to methodological errors in the analysis made by the CIA. He points out that the Soviet Union, for example, obtains a third of its sugar, half of its citrus fruit, and 40 percent of its cobalt and nickel from Cuba, thus making it difficult to imagine that it will be able to greatly alter its trade relations even as it enters the capitalist arena. The Soviet Union lacks hard currency with which it might buy these necessities

elsewhere, and Cuba seems willing to accept manufactured items of poor quality in trade. Meanwhile, Cuba is increasing its trade with other countries, particularly Latin America and China. Gunn concludes his analysis: "The political unrest, product of a severe but not catastrophic recession, can be contained. It is difficult to predict the effect of current and future reforms. If the majority of the population is sufficiently convinced that the downfall of socialism would bring with it the loss of those benefits that have come with the revolution, and if most maintain their support for Castro and aim their discontent at the inflexibility of the system rather than at a rejection of its ideology, then the program of reforms now being implemented will be capable of avoiding a massive uprising."

17. This and following data is from "Cuba navega con la historia" ("Cuba Navigates In Tune With History"), *Punto Final*, no. 250 (November 1991): 14-15, and "Caras nuevas en La Habana" ("New Faces in Havana"), *Punto Final* (Santiago, Chile), no. 253 (December 1991): 17. Of the twenty-five-member Politburo, three are women: Concepción Campa Huergo, María de los Angeles García Alvarez, and Yadira García Vera. It is interesting to note that Vilma Espín, president of the Federation of Cuban Women and until recently the only woman who was a full member of the Politburo, no longer figures among its members. She represents the old guard. The current female members are younger women who have come up through the ranks during these thirty-three years of revolutionary government

# CHAPTER 5

1. Alice Miller, *Breaking Down the Wall of Silence* (New York: Dutton, 1991), p. 142.

2. A number of therapeutic methods use this term. My own experience has been with a practitioner of Radix Therapy, one of the several schools influenced by the work of Wilhelm Reich. The theory is that incest and other traumas, often blocked and "forgotten" by the victim, live on in the fear or anger which has lodged itself in a particular part of the body. This "unremembered" fear or anger can and does cause disease, or "dis-ease." Body-memory work allows the victim to become a survivor, by understanding and dealing with the residue of unchanneled emotion.

3. Ruth Hubbard, *The Politics of Women's Biology* (New Brunswick, NJ: Rutgers University Press, 1990).

4. Elayne Rapping, "Self-help Bubble Drifts in Apolitical Ether," *The Guardian,* 6 May 1992. The full quote is: "While understandable as a response to a difficult political era, the recovery movement (useful, even life-saving as it may be for many in the most immediate sense) is, as a political philosophy, a mystifying diversion from reality. It has become a powerful social metaphor, focusing attention on our own victimization rather than our victimizers and on narcissistic efforts to 'heal ourselves' rather than change the world."

5. Literally "worm," the name Cuban revolutionaries have given to those who defect or otherwise betray the revolution.

6. Adrienne Rich, *Blood, Bread and Poetry—Selected Prose, 1979-1980* (New York: Norton, 1986). Term coined by the poet Adrienne Rich and analyzed in her essay "Compulsory Heterosexuality and the Lesbian Experience," 1980.

7. As if the increase in racist incidents across our country in recent years was not enough of a warning, the May 1992 verdict in the Rodney King case has shown us just how pivotal race hatred remains in our society. White police, videotaped beating a black motorist within inches of his life, were declared innocent of any wrongdoing. I do not find it surprising that the most coherent and political response to the Los Angeles riots was the document put forth by that city's two most powerful gangs, the Crips and the Bloods. United, they proposed billions in *effective* cleanup and reconstruction: for education, affordable housing, neighborhood health clinics, job training, and *forces of order that include community participation.* They demanded immediate consideration of their proposal, and implementation within four years. If this is done, they say, they will stop killing policemen and dealing drugs (they suggested that the money from the really big drug dealers be used to fund their program). It is not surprising that this important document has failed to receive much coverage in the media; and the FBI, in response, moved the majority of its operatives from the Mafia to the gangs.